GV
865
.P3
A3
1992

Paige, Leroy,
  1906-

Pitchin' man.

$29.50

DATE			
JAN 1994			

Pitchin' Man

Baseball and American Society
Series ISBN 0-88736-566-3

1. Blackball Stars
   John B. Holway
   ISBN 0-88736-094-7
   CIP 1988

2. Baseball History, Premier Edition
   Edited by Peter Levine
   ISBN 0-88736-288-5   1988

3. My 9 Innings: An Autobiography of 50 Years in Baseball
   Lee MacPhail
   ISBN 0-88736-387-3
   CIP 1989

4. Black Diamonds: Life in the Negro Leagues from the
   Men Who Lived It
   John B. Holway
   ISBN 0-88736-334-2
   CIP 1989

5. Baseball History 2
   Edited by Peter Levine
   ISBN 0-88736-342-3   1989

6. Josh and Satch: The Life and Times of Josh Gibson and
   Satchel Paige
   John B. Holway
   ISBN 0-88736-333-4
   CIP 1991

7. Encyclopedia of Major League Baseball Team Histories
   Edited by Peter C. Bjarkman
   Volume 1: American League
   ISBN 0-88736-373-3
   CIP 1991

8. Encyclopedia of Major League Baseball Team Histories
   Edited by Peter C. Bjarkman
   Volume 2: National League
   ISBN 0-88736-374-1
   CIP 1991

9. Baseball History 3
   Edited by Peter Levine
   ISBN 0-88736-577-9   1990

10. The Immortal Diamond: Baseball in American Literature
    Peter C. Bjarkman
    ISBN 0-88736-481-0 (hardcover)   CIP forthcoming,
    1992
    ISBN 0-88736-482-9 (softcover)   CIP forthcoming,
    1992

12. Baseball Players and Their Times: Oral Histories of the
    Game, 1920–1940
    Eugene Murdock
    ISBN 0-88736-235-4
    CIP 1991

13. The Tropic of Baseball: Baseball in the Dominican
    Republic
    Rob Ruck
    ISBN 0-88736-707-0
    CIP 1991

14. The Cinema of Baseball: Images of America, 1929–1989
    Gary E. Dickerson
    ISBN 0-88736-710-0
    CIP 1991

15. Baseball History 4
    Edited by Peter Levine
    ISBN 0-88736-578-7   1991

16. Baseball and American Society: A Textbook of Baseball
    History
    Peter C. Bjarkman
    ISBN 0-88736-483-7 (softcover)   CIP forthcoming,
    1992

17. Cooperstown Symposium on Baseball and the American
    Culture (1989)
    Edited by Alvin L. Hall
    ISBN 0-88736-719-4
    CIP 1991

18. Cooperstown Symposium on Baseball and the American
    Culture (1990)
    Edited by Alvin L. Hall
    ISBN 0-88736-735-6
    CIP 1991

19. Baseball Between the Wars: Memories of the Game
    by the Men Who Played It
    Eugene Murdock
    ISBN 0-88736-821-2
    CIP 1992

20. Pitchin' Man: Satchel Paige's Own Story
    Leroy Satchel Paige as told to Hal Lebovitz
    With a New Foreword by John B. Holway
    ISBN 0-88736-836-0
    CIP 1992

21. Cooperstown Symposium on Baseball and the American
    Culture (1991)
    Edited by Alvin L. Hall
    ISBN 0-88736-810-7   1992

22. My Greatest Memory in Baseball—Nostalgic Letters
    from Hall of Famers and Other Diamond Legends
    Edited by Peter C. Bjarkman
    ISBN 0-88736-804-2   CIP forthcoming, 1992

23. My Life in the Negro Leagues: An Autobiography
    Wilmer Fields
    With an Introduction by John B. Holway
    ISBN 0-88736-850-6
    CIP 1992

24. Biographical Encyclopedia of the Negro Leagues
    James A. Riley
    ISBN 0-88736-839-5   CIP forthcoming, 1992

25. Encyclopedia of Defunct Major League Teams
    Frederick Ivor-Campbell
    ISBN 0-88736-709-7   CIP forthcoming, 1993

26. The Hilldale Club: The History of a Negro League
    Baseball Team, 1910–1932
    Neil J. Lanctot
    ISBN 0-88736-864-6   CIP forthcoming, 1993

Pitchin' Man
Satchel Paige's Own Story

by
Leroy Satchel Paige
as told to
Hal Lebovitz

With a new Foreword by
John B. Holway

Meckler
Westport • London

Library of Congress Cataloging-in-Publication Data

Paige, Leroy, 1906–
    Pitchin' man : Satchel Paige's own story / Leroy Satchel Paige
as told to Hal Lebovitz ; with a new foreword by John B. Holway.
      p. cm. — (Baseball and American society ; 20)
    Reprint. Previously published: [Cleveland?], c1948.
    Includes index.
    ISBN 0-88736-836-0 (alk. paper) : $
    1. Paige, Leroy, 1906– . 2. Baseball players—United States—
Biography. 3. Pitchers (Baseball)—United States—Biography.
I. Lebovitz, Hal. II. Title. III. Series.
GV865.P3A3 1992
796.357'092—dc20
  [B]   92-5526
                                        CIP

British Library Cataloging-in-Publication Data is available.

Meckler Publishing, the publishing division of
  Meckler Corporation, 11 Ferry Lane West, Westport, CT 06880.
Meckler Ltd., 247-249 Vauxhall Bridge Road, London
  SW1V 1HQ, U.K.

Printed on acid free paper.
Printed and bound in the United States of America.

Publisher's Note

P itchin' Man: Satchel Paige's Own Story is reprinted exactly as originally published in 1948, first in the Cleveland *News,* and then in book form later that year. As N. R. Howard notes in his original Preface to the book, the reporting of Paige's words is a study in the vernacular, set down in an attempt to recreate the spirit and voice of the great ballplayer in conversation. As such, we feel that *Pitchin' Man* is a primary source document in the growing body of biographical work on Satchel Paige.

Contents

Foreword

"There were many Satchels," Satchel Paige told the audience at Cooperstown on his induction into the Hall of Fame in 1971.

He meant that there were many other great black players who also deserved recognition—and election to the shrine.

But his words were true in another sense too: In actuality, there were at least three Satchel Paiges.

One was the star pitcher of baseball legend.

Another was the droll humorist and minstrel show end-man.

The third was the least known of all, the revolutionary who helped effect a sea change in the game—and in American society as a whole. Jackie Robinson symbolized the revolution, but Satchel had been one of the crucial pioneers who helped force open the door so Jackie later could walk through.

Hal Lebovitz' delightful interview with the Great Man dwells in colorful detail on the first two Satchels. That's because neither Paige nor Lebovitz more than 40 years ago thought of the pitcher as a hero of what would later be called the civil rights movement. But, in his own way, he was.

In 1932 Satchel played in Negro League games a block away from Cleveland's League Park, where the white major league Indians played. He would later tell the ghost writer in his autobiography, *Maybe I'll Pitch Forever*, that he resented that the Indians and their park were closed to him.

Should Satch have protested publicly, raised a black fist, as the next generation of blacks—for instance, some 1968 Olympic champs—would?

Paige lived in a different world in 1932. The Ku Klux Klan still rode openly in the South, and reports of lynchings were not uncommon in the morning newspaper. Northern discrimination was less publicized and less bloody but equally real, as, of course, in many ways, it still is. Boys chose up sides by reciting, "Eeeny, meeny, miney, mo, catch a nigger by the toe." Amos 'n Andy on radio and Stepinfetchit in the movies kept the stereotypes alive. Newspaper stories routinely began with: "John Smith, 43, Negro, yesterday. . . ."

I believe that, given the climate of his times, if Paige had protested, he would have set off a reaction of anger that would have endangered not only him but the cause of all those like Robinson who would follow him. Baseball integration might have been set back for a decade or more.

Robinson, Willie Mays, Hank Aaron, Dave Winfield, Reggie Jackson—all have found fame and wealth in integrated baseball. Their good fortune was paid for by Paige and his generation, who spent thousands of nights bouncing over rural roads in the back seats of roadsters, their knees under their chins, or sleeping in third-rate hotels with the lights on to keep the bedbugs away.

Satch said he learned to pitch "by the hour. . . . Some places didn't want us in *town*, let alone the ball park, unless I pitched."

It's not that Satchel wasn't sensitive about discrimination. His teammate and manager on the Kansas City Monarchs, John "Buck" O'Neil, tells of standing silently with Paige before the old slave auction block in Charleston, South Carolina. At last Satch spoke up. "I feel like I been here before, roomie," he said. "Me too," O'Neil answered.

Paige made his protests with his arm. One of the most enduring anecdotes about him concerns the day in 1931 when he called in his fielders and struck out two big leaguers, Frank Demaree and Wallie Berger.

What the stories don't say is that he apparently pulled the stunt after hearing a racial catcall wafting out of the dugout or the stands.

Later, when Satch finally reached the major leagues himself, he objected to another racial epithet which he detected from Boston's erratic outfield star, Jimmy Piersall. Ordinarily Paige refused to throw at batters ("I don't call that no baseball if I have to cave your ribs in to get you"). But he made an exception for Piersall, asking how he'd like to hit "with the ball in your mouth." Said Satch later: "When he came up, he went down. He chased his hat and belt for two blocks."

This story of course is not in the Lebovitz interview, because it happened later, after Paige had joined the Browns.

Neither the writer nor the pitcher discussed Satchel's experiences winning acceptance on the Indians, perhaps because it was still too early to talk about such sensitive topics.

Larry Doby, another Negro Leaguer, who preceded Paige to Cleveland, reportedly objected to the pitcher's sense of humor, which he felt played to the white stereotypes of blacks, as did the Harlem Globe Trotters, for example. Satchel's old Monarchs teammate, Jackie Robinson, "detested" him for the same reason, according to Doby. Ironically, Robinson might not have been in the major leagues at all if Paige hadn't paved the way.

But Satchel's jokes helped to keep the team loose in a frantic pennant race.

His six victories helped even more, as the Indians ended up in a tie with the Red Sox. One less win from Satch, and Cleveland would have lost the flag. Paige's record for the year was 6–1, and his only loss came in relief against Boston as a result of two outfield misplays; he actually pitched better than the other Cleveland hurlers in the game, but he had the bad fortune to give up the go-ahead run.

Just as important was the stimulus Satchel gave to

the Cleveland attendance. In three straight starts, he
pitched before three sell-out crowds totaling 150,000
people—170,000 if you count those who crashed the
gate without tickets. Paige was one big reason why
Cleveland drew over two million that year, a record.

In spite of all his contributions, Paige was in the
doghouse with manager Lou Boudreau. He missed
everything, from bedchecks to airplanes to games,
and as punishment, he was benched for the final
month, and for the World Series.

I was in the upper stands behind home for the fifth
game of the Series, along with more than 78,000
other people, the all-time record major league crowd
at that time, when starter Bob Feller was knocked out
of the box. Would Satch come in? Out in the bullpen,
Paige was as anxious as the rest of us to hear his name
called. Instead, Boudreau called on two other fire-
men, as the opposition Boston Braves ran the score
up.

At last, in the seventh, after Boston had bombed
three pitchers for six runs in the inning, Paige was
called in. There were men on first and third and one
out. While the umpires fussed about his delivery—
they would call one balk against him—Satch gave up a
run-scoring fly and then got a double play to shut the
door.

But in later years he was still bitter at the slight.
They had left him in the bullpen "because of the color
of my skin, I guess." He never went back to
Cleveland. "And I'm not goin' back, either," he
vowed.

On the St. Louis Browns, Paige enjoyed the perks
due to a legend, reclining on a leather lounge chair in
the bullpen while winning an impressive 18 games
and saving 26 over three years for a tail-end club.

He gently inserted himself into the team poker
games on the train with a good-natured, "Any of you
boys call for a porter?"

His closest friend, Clint "Scrap Iron" Courtney of

Louisiana, worried what would happen if his father discovered the two of them together. Clint eventually relaxed, though. He figured that "me 'n Satch between us kin whup Pap."

Naturally, Paige was the first Negro Leaguer inducted into the Hall of Fame. Originally, the shrine planned to keep his plaque separate from those of the "big leaguers." But when critics pointed out that this smacked of "the back of the bus," Cooperstown relented and put Paige on the same wall with Bob Feller, Dizzy Dean, Ted Williams, and the other white stars he had pitched against and beaten.

Yet Paige never went back to Cooperstown either. The whites "thought we had tails," he said, "but we showed 'em." When he delivered his dictum that "there were many Satchels," Joe Reichler, an aide to commissioner Bowie Kuhn, told him to "sit down."

Satch not only sat down, he walked out—and never walked back.

So Satchel was not the clown he is often depicted as. He complained that the newspapers liked to pose him doing funny things and reported him mouthing funny quotes—his famous "Never look back, somethin' may be gainin' on you" was actually composed by a "sportin' writer from the East."

But life *was* fun for Satchel. As he discloses in these pages, he could even laugh at the hard knocks he took while growing up in Mobile, Alabama. (He does, however, fail to mention his interlude at reform school, where, among other things, he learned some refinements on his baseball skills, an experience not unlike that of Babe Ruth.)

His teammate, Chet Brewer, told of Satchel's notorious driving habits: making U-turns across pedestrian islands, weaving in and out among on-coming cars on one-way streets, leading traffic cops on 90-mph chases across the California landscape. Some policemen, learning who he was, tore up the tickets, turned on their sirens, and escorted him to the park

just as the irate fans were about to murder the pro-
moters.

Paige loved fast cars and fast women; his tastes in
both were gargantuan. O'Neil tells of Satchel sneak-
ing two girls into a hotel in adjoining rooms. He
tiptoed out of one room and rapped softly on the
door of the other, calling, "Nancy? Nancy?" as softly
as he could. When the first door flew open and an
irate woman demanded to know who Nancy was,
O'Neil, hearing the commotion, sleepily opened a
third door. Sizing the situation up, he piped up,
"Yeah, Satch, what you want?" Thereafter, O'Neil was
known to the pitcher as Nancy.

Paige gave everyone nicknames. Brewer was
Dooflackem; Whitey Herzog, his minor-league teammate, was Wild Child, etc. Even his pitches had nicknames—the be ball, the bat dodger, the four-day
rider, the midnight creeper, etc. Whatever they were
called, his catcher, Joe Greene, grinned, they were all
high hard ones. Satch didn't learn a curve until late in
life—and didn't have to.

Satch could pitch, of course. Joe DiMaggio, still a
minor leaguer, singled off him in San Francisco in
1935 and was overjoyed. "I know I can make the
majors now," he said.

Paige had many a duel against white stars Dizzy
Dean and Bobby Feller. Dean always said Satchel was
the best he ever saw, "and I been lookin' in the mirror
a long time."

Paige's greatest rival was Josh Gibson, the legend-
ary black slugger. They had once been battery-mates
on the Pittsburgh Crawfords; *that* must have been the
greatest battery in baseball history!

By 1942 they were in opposite leagues, Paige on the
western Kansas City Monarchs and Gibson on the
eastern Homestead Grays. Gibson spread the word
that he hoped to catch Satchel with the bases loaded
some day. "Blab, blab, blab," Paige mimicked.

They met in the Negro League World Series that

year, and Satch deliberately walked the bases loaded to bring up Josh. "I'm gonna feed you nothin' but fastballs," he announced, and struck Josh out on three of them, sidearm at the knees.

No man has ever hit .400 since Paige and other blacks entered the so-called "major leagues." The feat had once been quite common, "but I'd have taken something off those fat batting averages," Satch declared.

Ted Williams marveled at Paige's nice easy motion, and while he was marveling he was going 1-for-6 in the batters' box. On the seventh try, Satch got two strikes against Ted, took his stretch on the mound, and lifted a finger off the ball. "Jesus, curve," Ted told himself. Instead the fast ball whooshed over, strike three.

Next day Paige arrived late, as usual, during the National Anthem. Bursting into the Red Sox dugout, he demanded to know, "Where's Ted at? Where's Ted at?"

"Right here, Satch," Williams answered.

"Man," Paige guffawed, "You ought to know better than to guess with old Satchel!"

Still, there were those who insisted that Paige's signing with Cleveland in '48 was just another of owner Bill Veeck's publicity stunts. When Satch was voted rookie of the year at the age of 44, he wondered which year they meant—he had broken in with the Birmingham Black Barons back in 1927.

He helped pitch his club to the second-half pennant that season with an 8–3 record and followed that with 12–4 for a second-division club the next year. (Negro League seasons were about half as long as major league schedules.) In '28 Paige set a Negro League record with 184 strikeouts in 196 innings, a mark that was never broken. He also holds the lifetime strikeout mark. Satch would have his best year— 13–3—in 1934 with the Crawfords.

After a year on the North Dakota prairies hurling

for a white semipro team, Satch went to Mexico and
suddenly lost his golden arm. He couldn't raise his
hand above his shoulder. The owner of the Kansas
City Monarchs, J. L. Wilkinson, hired him as a coach
on his traveling "B" team, and the arm miraculously
came back, with the help, perhaps, of a secret Indian
snake oil potion he had received from an Indian girl
in the Dakotas.

Satchel started pitching two and three innings a
night to draw the crowds, which depressed his victory
totals but made him a pile of money, up to $40,000 a
year by some estimates. If these are accurate, Paige
was the highest-paid player in America, making more
even than Lou Gehrig, Joe DiMaggio, Jimmy Foxx,
Bob Feller, Lefty Grove, or Hank Greenberg.

At last the white world discovered Satch. *Time* Mag-
azine hailed him as "one of the greatest pitchers of
any hue in baseball history." *Life* did a picture spread,
and *The Saturday Evening Post* called him "the Choco-
late Rube Waddell," after another eccentric strikeout
artist who had also called in his fielders and struck out
the side. The *Post* article was filled with what today
would be considered stereotype racial language. But
no matter. Satch was suddenly a star, on a pedestal
alongside Olympic star Jesse Owens and heavyweight
champ Joe Louis.

Crowds flocked to see Satchel. Where once he had
drawn 3,000 fans, he now drew ten times as many in
every city he visited. After a decade of Depression,
Paige began to haul the black teams out of the red ink.
"He made the payroll for a lot of clubs," Buck O'Neil
says.

"Even the white folks were coming out," Paige
wrote. "They heard about Josh and me." Thanks to
the two superstars, "everyone ate lean meat."

When Paige pitched against Dizzy Dean in Chicago's Wrigley Field in 1942, they outdrew a White
Sox double header by 8,000 fans.

The East-West, or annual All Star showcase for

black players, drew 50,000 to Comiskey Park. Future
baseball commissioner Ford Frick joined the throng
and predicted that the doors to the majors might
open after all.

In 1942 rumors grew insistent. Singer Paul
Robeson pleaded with the white owners to "have a
heart." Brooklyn manager Leo Durocher said he's
seen "a million good . . . colored boys." When commissioner Kenesaw Mountain Landis called Leo into
the woodhouse for a spanking, Leo emerged saying
he was "misquoted," and Landis piously said there
was no rule, "subterranean or otherwise," keeping
blacks out of the majors. "One hundred percent hy-
pocrisy!" snorted Yankee owner Larry MacPhail, who
nevertheless joined the other owners in barring
blacks. ("There's just too many of you," A's owner
Connie Mack had told the black third base star, Judy
Johnson.)

Paige himself suggested that, if the whites wouldn't
play on the same team with blacks, why not form an
all-black team for the majors: Bill Veeck actually tried
to carry out such a plan with the woeful Philadelphia
Phils' franchise until Landis shot the idea down.

Nevertheless, several teams reportedly did offer
tryouts to black stars such as Roy Campanella and a
college football star named Jackie Robinson. Paige, at
38, was ignored as too old. In the end, nothing came
of it, of course, and Paige returned to the Monarchs
and the all-night bus rides. What a shame that he—
plus Gibson, Campanella, Robinson *et al.*—didn't
come up then. What records they might have written!
If Paige was great in '48, what would he have done six
years earlier? The majors were about to hire a one-
arm pitcher to fill their wartime rosters. But they
weren't ready yet to hire a two-arm black.

Satch meantime struck a blow for higher pay for
the other players. They had been getting $50 a man
for playing in the East-West Game. Josh and Satch
decided to hold out for $200, which they were

grudgingly given, and the following year the other players got a similar raise.

In 1944 Paige visited wounded GIs back from the Pacific, many of whom had seen him play. The experience moved him very much, and he proposed that the East-West Game be played as a benefit for them. The owners refused, so Paige boycotted the affair, a stance for which he was roundly vilified in the black press.

The following year I myself joined a throng of 30,000 mostly black fans who packed Washington's Griffith Stadium to see Satchel pitch against Gibson and the Grays. I still remember his windmill windup, reminiscent of comedian Joe E. Brown in the movie *Elmer the Great.* Neither Paige nor I, nor anyone else there that night suspected that, within a few short months, a black man would be hired by the Brooklyn Dodgers and that baseball—and America—would be transformed forever.

Why Jackie Robinson? Why not Paige and Gibson? A broken-hearted Paige groped for answers. "It was my right," he wrote in *Maybe I'll Pitch Forever.* "I got those white boys thinking. . . ."

But Robinson is good, Satchel's wife, Lahoma, consoled him.

"He's no Satchel Paige," the wounded pitcher shot back.

While Robinson stole all the headlines at the Dodger farm team in Montreal, the forgotten Paige had a good year, 5-1, with the Monarchs. That fall he took his frustration out barnstorming against his old friend and foe, Bob Feller, who had an all-star white squad. The Paiges won six of the 13 games. In their personal duel, Satchel outpitched Bobby. He allowed 1.73 runs per nine innings, compared to 2.73 for Feller. Satchel gave the white stars a .159 batting average; the blacks hit Bob for a .235 average.

In 1947 the Negro Leagues "couldn't even draw flies," in the words of old-time star Buck Leonard. Paige bumped around the prairies, winning one and losing one, and almost ready to quit the game. He wrote to Veeck, asking for a job with the Indians, but the Cleveland boss turned him down.

Finally, in 1948 the long-awaited telegram came, and Satchel Paige entered the major leagues. That's where Hal Lebovitz met him and recorded the interview that became this charming book.

Paige's old catcher, James "Joe" Greene, told me: "I still say we did a lot for baseball, even if nobody knows about us any more. They say Jackie paved the way. He didn't pave the way. We did."

The White Sox' Minnie Minoso, who started out in the Negro Leagues, agreed. "Everything I have," he once said, "I owe to you guys."

"You were the pioneers," Willie Mays told Satchel at an old-timers' reunion in 1981. "You made it possible for us."

Eric "Ric" Roberts, long-time sports columnist for the black Pittsburgh *Courier,* tried to put Paige's contribution into words. "Satchel Paige led us into the promised land," Roberts said. "He was the guy gave black baseball its first real financial solvency. We won't see his like again in our lifetime."

—John B. Holway
1992

Preface
to the 1948 Edition

As far as we at the Cleveland *News* can determine, nothing has ever appeared in print, in all the annals of American literature, like this vernacular autobiography of a great American baseball player. Satchel Paige will be set down by history as one of the game's best. His know-how of baseball, sandwiched between gleeful reminiscences of a career of ball-playing all over the western hemisphere, will instantly catch the fancy of any lover of the national pastime.

But Satchel Paige is no literary performer. The idea of the worthiness-in-print of his years of "fireball" pitching, apparently, had not occurred to him before Hal Lebovitz of the *News'* sports staff interested him in the Paige Saga and offered to set it down himself, as expert biographer, if Satchel would just talk it out.

When these fitful chapters of a life both hilarious and sport-important appeared serially in the *News* (a few have been added) the reader reaction quickly convinced us that here was something *new* in lives of the great ones.

It was offered then and now as the actual words and reflections as they came from Satchel Paige just as he talked. The reader is hereby notified that if he likes these words they are just as they came from a singular athlete and person, and that if he disapproves of any of them they still are the words of Satchel himself. Satch's immense value to the Indians this season may give the words added luster.

N. R. Howard
Editor, The News

Foreword
to the 1948 Edition

"Say, I'll come to Cleveland and show you. I'm the best pitcher in baseball."

That's a pretty brave statement coming from anyone, even the fabulous Negro pitcher, Satchel Paige, long known as a master of overstatement when referring to his talents on the mound.

But if he didn't prove he is the best pitcher today, he conclusively demonstrated what everyone has long suspected, that he undoubtedly was the best, one, two, or three decades ago.

My introduction to Paige was unusual, of course. Here was this long, stringy Negro of indeterminate age, trotting around the park "getting in shape," entirely unimpressed by the coming test which might insure his advent into major league baseball after a twenty-year wait. Unconcerned, he strolled to the mound. Twenty minutes later, after throwing fifty pitches to the American League's second best batsman, Manager Lou Boudreau (only four were not over the plate and he apologized for his lack of control), he strolled back, perfectly certain that finally he had made the grade.

Everything in my association with Satch since has been unusual. He is a most remarkable fellow and one who is very nearly the most remarkable athlete of our time.

He is a personality as interesting off the field as on. And by the figures, baseball's greatest drawing card— a character that defies complete transference to paper but one about whom many books can and will be written.

Bill Veeck,
President, Cleveland Baseball Corporation

From Lou Boudreau

S atchel Paige's own story is easily the most amusing autobiography I ever have read—but it is considerably more than that.

Between the lines of this rollicking chronicle by and about a fellow who developed the "hesitation" pitch while fighting his way with rocks to his favorite swimming hole, the reader will discover a more serious pattern, the story of a man who made his way from poverty and obscurity to become one of the greatest box office attractions in baseball history.

I am interested in Paige mainly as a pitcher for the Cleveland Indians. In that capacity he has been spectacularly successful. Whatever his mysterious age, Old Satch is a wonder. There is no doubt in my mind that at his peak he must have ranked with the Walter Johnsons, Christy Mathewsons and Bob Fellers among the greatest pitchers of all time.

Personally, he is a refreshing combination of on-the-field earnestness and off-the-field good humor. All of us Indians have enjoyed having him with us. You'll enjoy having him with you—in this, his own story.

Lou Boudreau
Manager, Cleveland Indians
1948

Introduction
to the 1948 Edition

This is being written just after the announcer at Cleveland Stadium reported a new record night crowd of 78,382 had overflowed grandstand, bleachers, and into the field to see the Cleveland Indians battle the last place Chicago White Sox.

At least half the crowd was there to see Satchel Paige. He had been announced as the starting pitcher and the magnetism of his name sold the ducats.

It was merely a repeat performance of what occurred when old Satch started against Washington a few weeks earlier. And only seven days before when the fans jammed Comiskey Park Chicago so severely that two gates were smashed.

No other player since Babe Ruth had the crowd appeal Old Satch possesses. Obviously the oddity of an old man doing the impossible—handcuffing major leaguers—makes Satch a box office sensation.

Similarly it was the unusual—Babe Ruth's home run punch—which previously had captivated the fans. But it was more than that. It was Ruth the person—his walk, his easy manner with a buck, his inability to remember names, his refusal to take orders, his prodigious appetite, his touch for the theatrical, performing the sensational at the proper psychological moment—these made Ruth the personality, the "Babe," the crowd-pleaser.

So it is with Paige.

No one called Ruth "George," just as no one calls Paige "Leroy." Paige wouldn't answer if they did. He signs his checks "Satchel." His autograph reads "Satchel Paige."

Like Ruth, he is a non-conformist. He does as he doggone pleases. He disregards appointments, calendars or time-pieces. He makes dates, then forgets about them. Fact is, he has difficulty remembering his pitching assignments.

He doesn't mean to break his engagements. He simply can't say "No."

When someone asks, "Will you come to my house for dinner tonight?" Satch automatically answers "Okay." Chances are he has said "Okay" to ten similar invitations.

But it's impossible to become angry at Satch. A smile, a humorous remark, and the broken date is forgotten. He means well. He simply possesses the chronic inability to keep appointments.

I have seen him keep big-wigs waiting hours while he signs autographs for the small fry.

His sense of humor, coupled with his quaint, ungrammatical expressions, make him personable to the extreme. Satch doesn't "open up" immediately to interviewers, but once he warms up, he captivates his audience. He always has a laugh provoking answer.

Satch, like Ruth, has difficulty remembering names. It took him a week after signing an Indians' contract to learn Bill Veeck's name. He kept referring to the Indians' president as "That curly-haired fellow in the front office."

He says Veeck is one of the greatest men he has ever met. "I'm gonna pitch my arm off for that fellow," he has often told me.

He rarely knows the name of the batter he's facing. Neither excitement nor worry seems to be part of his personality. From his walk to his windups, he appears to be a picture of relaxation.

However, he is sensitive. He was perturbed by a story which claimed some of his Indians' teammates were unfriendly to him. The story was completely untrue. His teammates were the first to deny the printed piece. They enjoy his humor and have a deep respect for his ability. But Satch was irked, "Now why would somebody want to write something like that?" he kept asking.

In collaborating with Satchel in writing these chapters, I tried to record the incidents as he revealed them to me, and in his own language. Just as Dizzy Dean has his own peculiar well-publicized grammar, so has Paige and it is an important part of his personality.

Cy Slapnicka, the scout who discovered Bob Feller, saw Paige pitch in the Wichita tournament in 1935. "At that time," says Cy, "He was as great as any pitcher I have ever seen."

Now, thirteen years later he is still SOME pitcher.

And unquestionably he has lost none of his magnetic crowd-appealing personality—the greatest in the majors.

Hal Lebovitz
Friday August 20, 1948

1
Home Plate Don't Move

Mr. Lou Boudreau signaled me from the bull pen that night, July 9, 1948 it was, against the St. Louis Browns in Cleveland Stadium. Was I nervous? Well I wasn't nervous exactly, but I was as close to that feelin' as I could be. I never had a feelin' like it before. 'Course I had never pitched in the majors before.

It was a long walk from the Stadium bull pen to the pitchin' rubber and I knew all those folks in the stands were studying me. I don't mind that. Folks has been eyeing me all my life. But these folks were different. I could feel it. They were sort of like people at a circus. They were asking themselves, "Can that old man really pitch?"

• • •

I'm not so old, but I knew they'd be ready to laugh at Mr. Bill Veeck [see Appendix B] if I didn't make good.

• • •

"And how about me?" I asked myself. Am I playing the fool? I know I can pitch. I been stopping major leaguers all my life. But this was different. This was for keeps. One mistake, a wrong pitch or two and my bubble would go plop. My work would be over—just when I wanted it to start.

So when I got to that rubber, I sure felt funny. I had a kind of a heavy pressure. I had been in many serious spots before, but this was MOST serious. Those flash bulbs popping all about me told me that.

• • •

Mr. Boudreau came up to me. He said, "Satch, you've got nothing to fear. Don't be scared if they hit you. Pitch loose like you always do."

• • •

Mr. Boudreau's speech gave me a lot of encouragement.

The first batter did hit me. Chuck Stevens, I think it was. He sent a single to left. The hit kind of woke me.

"Look Satch," I said to myself, "you've been here before."

Sure enough, I had been. I was the first colored pitcher ever to throw in the Stadium. That was right after they built the place and I was playing with the Pittsburgh Crawfords.

There was home plate where it always was. You know home plate is home plate regardless where you play. It don't move.

• • •

That's all there was to it. I used my single windup, my double windup, my triple windup, my hesitation windup—and my no windup. I used my step-n-pitch-it, my sidearm throw, and my bat dodger. The Browns didn't do no damage in the two innings I worked.

• • •

Next time, when I went against the Brooklyn Dodgers, July 14, in the exhibition for the sandlot boys, there were 65,000 in the stands. I played in front of big crowds before but this was the biggest. Still, I didn't have any special feelings. The first pressure was over, y' understand.

The crowd was surprised when I struck out the side. I wasn't, I did that lots of times. And I expect to do it more, too.

First Major League Appearance
July 9, 1948

St. Louis	A	H	O	A		CLEVE.	A	H	O	A
Dillinger,3b	4	1	3	3		Mitchell,lf	5	1	1	0
Stevens,1b	4	2	11	0		Ber'dino,1b	5	0	6	1
Priddy,2b	2	1	4	4		Edwards,rf	5	1	3	0
Platt,lf	3	1	5	0		Boudreau,ss	5	1	2	3
Zarilla,cf-rf	4	0	1	0		Gordon,2b	3	3	5	2
Kokos,rf	2	1	0	0		Keltner,3b	4	1	0	2
Lehner,cf	0	0	1	0		Judnich,cf	4	3	3	0
Partee,c	4	1	1	2		Hegan,c	4	1	7	1
Pellagrini,ss	4	0	1	6		Lemin,p	1	0	0	3
Sanford,p	3	2	0	2		Paige,p	0	0	0	0
Garver,p	1	0	0	0		*Peck	0	0	0	0
						†Doby	1	1	0	0
Totals	31	9	27	17		‡Kennedy	0	0	0	0
						Klieman,p	0	0	0	0
						¶Tucker	1	0	0	0
						Gromek,p	0	0	0	0
						Totals	38	12	27	12

*Walked for Lemon in fourth.
†Singled for Paige in sixth.
‡Ran for Doby in sixth.
¶Grounded out for Klieman in eighth.

St. Louis .... 3 1 0 0 0 0 1 0 0—5
CLEVELAND ... 1 0 0 0 0 1 1 0 0—3

Runs—Priddy, Platt, Zarilla, Sanford 2, Mitchell, Gordon, Judnich. Errors—Sanford, Judnich.
Runs batted in—Kokos, Partee 2, Boudreau, Sanford, Doby, Platt, Keltner. Two-base hits—Hegan, Judnich, Keltner. Three-base hit—Judnich. Home run—Sanford. Stolen base—Dillinger. Sacrifices—Priddy, Dillinger, Stevens. Double plays—Pellagrini, Priddy and Stevens; Gordon and Boudreau; Gordon, Boudreau and Berardino. Left on bases—St. Louis 7, Cleveland 10. bases on balls—Sanford 2, Lemon 2, Klieman 2, Gromek 1. Struck out—Paige 1, Gromek 1, Lemon 2, Garver 2. Hits—Lemon 5 in 4; Paige, 2 in 2; Klieman, 1 in 2; Gromek, 1 in 1; Sanford, 12 in 6⅔; Garver, none in 2⅓. Passed ball—Partee. Winner—Sanford. Loser—Lemon.

Many folks don't realize that I took a chance signing with the Cleveland Indians. You see I had a pretty good financial thing with the Kansas City Monarchs and the barnstorming. Now supposing I didn't make good in the big leagues. That would make me a poor draw if I went back to the barnstorming.

• • •

I really wasn't gambling, though. You don't gamble when you has confidence, and that's what I got. I knew I could outsmart batters. I knew I could help the Indians.

. . .

I wanted to help them last summer. I wired Mr. Bill Veeck the boss, and told him so. He replied, "No." He said he was afraid if he signed me then the fans would think he was doing it to help the gate. He didn't want folks to think that.

This year Mr. Veeck didn't need a special gate attraction. More than a million had paid to see the team before I joined up. Fact is, he was sure of over two million through advance orders before he signed me.

He didn't need me as no gate attraction. He needed me to help win the pennant.

He looked all over the country for another pitcher before he came to me. He got Sam Zoldak from the Browns just before the trading deadline and I'm told he sent his scouts to shake every bush but they found no berries.

Then Abe Saperstein, who scouts colored talent for the Indians and happens to be a close friend of mine, asked Mr. Veeck, "Why don't you sign Satch?"

"Is he available?" asked Mr. Veeck. Abe thought I was.

Mr. Veeck said, "Let me think it over."

Then Mr. Veeck talked to Bob Rapid Feller, Joe Gordon, Kenny Keltner, Johnny Berardino and Bob Lemon. Those are the Cleveland boys I pitched against on Bob Rapid Feller's barnstorming trip on the coast last fall.

. . .

They said, "Snatch Satch. He's better than anybody you can get."

. . .

Mr. Veeck talked to Mr. Boudreau, the manager. He felt the same way.

Still Mr. Veeck wasn't convinced. He had seen me pitch about 25 times, but the last time was back in 1934 when I beat Dizzy Dean's team, 1–0, in a 13-inning game on the coast.

Mr. Veeck called Mr. Saperstein. He asked Abe, "How do I know Satch is still in good shape?"

"I'll bring him down and you'll see," replied Abe.

So I came to Cleveland and had a meeting with Mr. Veeck and Mr. Boudreau.

Mr. Boudreau said to me, "What we're looking for is a fellow who can get the ball over the plate all the time so the batter can put some wood on it—but not too much wood."

I said, "Look, Mr. Boudreau, I'll do anythin' you want. I'll go out on the field in my street clothes and pitch. You can see for yourself. If I'm no good I'll buy my own train ticket out of here. You're under no obligation."

We went down to the Stadium field, Hank Greenberg was there. He's a vice president. He watched. So did Mr. Veeck. Mr. Boudreau and I both put on uniforms and I pitched to him.

• • •

I threw 50 pitches. Only four missed the strike zone.

• • •

I guess the Indians found their man because they offered me a contract.

Mr. Veeck asked, "How much did you expect to make this year in baseball?" I didn't have no adding machine but I gave him a rough amount.

Mr. Veeck said, "Okay. We'll give you more than that." He named a much smoother figure.

• • •

I signed—FAST!

2
About My Age

Now about my age. That's usually a subject for women but I guess we got to go into it because the way everybody is fussin' it seems it's as important as the secret of the atomic bomb.

I read a headline the other day, "Satchel's Age— The $64 Question." The way things are going now pretty soon they'll be givin' wash machines, vacuum cleaners, automobiles and a year's vacation 'round the world for the right answer.

Before we study into this I want everybody to understand one thing. If I'm a little fuzzy about some of the dates in my life it's because I always got a problem a whole lot bigger to conjure with. I got to keep thinkin' of my pitchin'.

• • •

Take for instance that fellow with the Philadelphia Athletics, Majeski. He hit a home run off me. So did Dee DiMaggio in Boston. Now, how did they do that? That's what I got to think about. I made a mistake somewhere. And I got to figure out what it was. This I know for sure. They won't EVER get pitches again like they got.

• • •

And I got to learn about all the other batters, too. Now how can a man concentrate on dates and such when he's got a much bigger problem? So excuse me if I'm a little bit fuzzy about what year this was or that was, won't you, please?

All right, back to my age.

My ex-wife Janet—I married her 15 years ago—

told the newspapers I was born July 28, 1905. She says she saw it in my mother's home, down in Mobile, Alabama, in the family Bible. Let's see, 1905. That would make me 43.

• • •

Now also according to the newspapers my mother says I'm 44, and she's got the Bible right there in Mobile. It's the same Bible and even it don't have me clear.

• • •

My mother didn't tell nobody my age. She had eleven children. How can she keep track of all them birthdays?

A judge in California says I'm 48. He says I was 41 about seven years ago when I was arrested for speeding. I suppose you gotta believe a judge.

I can show you a man who says I'm over 60. Everybody's got a different number. They play bingo with me.

When I was travelin' with the Kansas City Monarchs the folks in the stands would bet. Not on the game but on my age. All the money would go into a pool. Then someone would come down and ask me. Person closest would get the pot.

Sports writers always ask my age. Nobody believes the right number when they do read it. I tell 'em I'm 45 or 50 or 60—whatever they want me to tell 'em. I suppose, when you come down to it, it's my fault everybody thinks I'm so old. They want me to be old so I give 'em what they want. Seems they get a bigger kick out of an old man throwing strikeouts.

• • •

When I was in New York with the Indians the sports writers begged me for my real age. I told them 41. If I told them I was below that they'd laugh. Just like you're going to laugh when I tell you I have just come round to 40.

• • •

My draft card says I was born September 18, 1908, and that's speaking fact.

Now just ask yourself, how can a man pitch hard and pitch every day like I been doin' if he's old? Could I be 50 and doin' what I'm doin' now?

Mr. Bill Veeck and Mr. Boudreau say they don't care if I'm 99 or 199 as long as I can pitch. Ain't that the important thing?

But it kind of hurts me when folks say I'm an old man.

Jack Benny says he's 38. Well, I'll go two better.

Now don't forget. My birthday was September 18. That made me 40. Isn't that where life begins?

• • •

I'll have to tell my arm.

3
Everybody Wants Clews

You hear all kinds of stories about how long I been pitchin'. One fellow says he saw me pitch professional baseball way back in 1916. Another says he saw me pitch in 1910.

Now this is real fact. I was 17 when I signed with the Chattanooga Black Lookouts of the Southern Association and pitched my first professional baseball. It always seemed to me I signed in 1927.

I was so sure it was '27 that I told a sports reporter of the Cleveland *News* that I would pay the first person who could find a clippin'—any scrap of paper— provin' I played professional baseball before '27 a reward of $500.

Man, that really started somethin'. Offerin' that $500 set lotsa folks workin' and thinkin'.

Some fellow called up and said he saw me pitch against Smoky Joe Williams of the Homestead Grays back in 1920. "Get the clippin'" I told him. He said he was hurryin' down to Homestead, Pa. immediately to seek out the back papers.

I told him to speed. Five hundred dollars was waitin'.

When I walked down the street everybody waved the *News* at me. "Give us some clews, Satchel," they was askin'.

One big fellow said he was goin' to stop in the Crawford Grill in Pittsburgh and see Gus Greenlee, my old manager. "Gus got plenty of clippins'. Get that $500 ready," he said.

• • •

I didn't scare. The $500 was ready but Gus

wouldn't help him. Ain't no such clippin' in the Crawford Grill.

. . .

One morning 'bout 10 fellows came into my room at the Majestic Hotel. "We been arguin' about your age, Satchel and we come up here lookin' for clews," they said.

"Look all you want," I told 'em, "Ain't no clews here."

One fellow said, "Take off your bathrobe. I want to examine you."

I did. He felt the skin on my back, my arms and my chest. "Skin like a baby's," he said. "Skin's no clew."

. . .

"Open your mouth," a boy said. He looked in. "No evidence there," he agreed.

. . .

Another fellow said, "Let me see your eyes."

I looked straight at him. He lifted my eyebrows and eyelids. He made me squint left 'n right. He looked deep down in me.

"No spots there. Can't tell your age from your peepers," he said.

"Bend down. Let's see your hair," a couple of the boys asked me.

I did and they peeked all around.

. . .

"Imagine, Satch ain't got a gray hair. Say you is ageless. No clews here."

. . .

As they left I heard one of the boys remark, "Maybe that Satch was a leap year baby."

. . .

Everybody laughed. So did I. I still had the $500.

4
Expensive Sleep

I suppose you're wonderin' if I ever paid that $500. Well, I did. A Cleveland fellow, livin' on the west side of town trapped me. Lotsa folks tried but only the west side fellow got me in a corner and I hadda dig deep.

A coupla folks tried to collect by showin' me a book called *They Played the Game*. The author, Harry Grayson, did me honor by puttin' in a chapter about me. But he didn't do me no honor when he said in print, right on page 133, I played semi-professional baseball starting in 1920.

• • •

Ain't that a laugh. That Harry Grayson musta got that number out 'o some old grab bag. Maybe he was listenin' to that Gabriel Heatter who said on the radio in a voice soundin' like someone was dyin', "Ladies and Gentlemen, ah yes, ah yes, Satchel Paige, Satchel Paige. The man who has been 40 for the last 15 years."

• • •

And then I got this telegram:

Satchel Paige:
When I played third base for Dallas team in Texas League in 1912 and 1913 you pitched for Fort Worth so bring that Five Hundred down to the Hollenden Hotel, Cleveland. If you don't see me around the lobby you can leave it with my friend Henry Jones at Bell Captain's desk.
(Signed)
Charles Time-Clock Hubbell

That fellow didn't want much. All he wanted was his name in print.

• • •

Well, he got it.

• • •

But this Cleveland west side fellow, he didn't bring me nothin' phony. He come 'round with a photostatic copy from the sportin' page from the Memphis *Commercial Appeal*, dated May 17, 1926.

On the bottom of the page was a box score of a game between the Chattanooga Lookouts and the Memphis Red Sox. Pitchin' for the Lookouts was a pitcher by the name of "Satchell."

Now when I first was taken into professional baseball I was called "Satchell"—spelled just like that. It wasn't 'till I proved myself that they wrote me down as "Paige."

But I was sure the "Satchell" in that Memphis box score couldn't be me and I hadda unprove it. I know that Charley Askew of the colored Y.M.C.A. in Birmingham has records showin' another boy called "Satchell" was pitchin' 'round there in '26.

• • •

I have a clippin' from Cuba showin' I pitched there last year and I never was near that hot spot in '47. But a clippin' says I was. Which shows you can't always trust printin'.

• • •

Well, when this west side fellow come 'round with the photostat showin' I was down in Memphis in '26, like they say in court the burden of proof was on me. It was me who made the offer of $500 to the first person showin' a clippin' that I played professional ball before '27.

The Memphis Red Sox won the second game of the series from the Chattanooga club yesterday, 4 to 3, at Lewis Park.

Augustus, Sox pitcher, permitted three hits up to the seventh, when he weakened and was found for four.

The Sox won in the final inning, when Walker was hit and scored on Ward's hit.

Augustus fanned seven men and Satchell, Chattanooga hurler, three.

The same teams play today and Tuesday. The score:

CHATTANOOGA.	ab.	r.	h.	o.	a.	MEMPHIS.	ab.	r.	h.	o.	a.
Lowe, 3b	4	1	2	3	2	Ward cf	4	0	2	0	0
Cooper lf	5	0	1	2	0	Moore lf	3	1	0	1	0
Cleags rf	5	0	0	0	0	Wesley rf	2	0	1	0	0
Gurley cf	2	0	0	1	0	Russ ss	4	1	2	2	2
Mitchell ss	4	0	0	1	1	Miller 2b	3	0	1	1	4
Stone c	4	0	2	3	4	M'Has'l 1b	4	1	1	13	1
Herman 2b	3	0	0	3	2	Bufford 3b	4	0	0	1	1
Lev'wn 1b	3	2	2	11	0	Walker c	3	1	1	3	2
Satchell p	4	0	0	0	3	Augustus p	3	0	0	0	3
						Glass rf	1	0	1	1	0
Totals	34	3	7x	24	12	Totals	32	4	9	27	13

x—None out when winning run scored.

By Innings—
Chattanooga . . . . . . .0 0 1 0 0 0 1 0 1—3
Memphis . . . . .1 1 0 0 0 0 1 1—4

Summary: Errors—Levanshown, Miller. Two-base hits—Cooper, Miller, Lowe. Three-base hits—McHaskell, Walker, Levanshown. Sacrifice hits—Herman, Augustus. Stolen bases—Lowe, Gurley, Moore, Wesley, Russ 2. Double play—McHaskell to Walker to Bufford. Left on bases—Chattanooga 9, Memphis 7. Bases on balls—Off Satchell 3, off Augustus 4. Struck out—By Satchell 3, by Augustus 7. Hit by pitcher—Walker. Umpires—Cummins and Sharkey. Time 2:15.

The $500 clipping from the Memphis Commercial Appeal, *May 17, 1926.*

How the west side fellow got the clippin' was through his sister. This west side fellow was down in Memphis visitin' his sister and her husband and they starts talkin' about me 'cause the Indians had just signed me up. This sister's husband says he seen me pitchin' in the South way back when.

The west side fellow—his name is Carl Goerz—

thinks nothin' about it 'till he comes home and sees my reward offer in the Cleveland *News*.

. . .

Right off he calls up his sister long distance and says "Hunt up all the old newspaper files and let's make this fool cough up that $500."

. . .

Guess his sister traipsed all around that Memphis town 'till she found one single, lonely paper, in the public library with the name "Satchell" in the box score. Knowin' that was my nickname, she got some photostatin' people to make a copy and she mailed it up north to her brother.

He shows me the clippin'. I say, "It can't be me 'cause I didn't start 'till '27."

He says, "Ha ha! Prove it."

I say, "There's only one man who can unprove that clippin'. His name is Alex Herman. Alex is the man who carried me into baseball. He signed me to my first professional contract wtih Chattanooga. I'll ask him to write me the truth, even if it hurts."

Well, it did hurt—to the pain of $500. Alex wrote back: "It is true beyond all contradiction that I gave Satchel his first chance to play professional baseball. I was the owner of the Chattanooga Black Lookouts of the Southern Association. It was in April 1926 that I carried him to Chattanooga for spring training . . . ." [A reprint of Alex Herman's letter will be found in Appendix A.]

There it was. Right from Alex. I looked at his letter—and looked and looked. I couldn't believe it, but there it was. 'Til that moment I always believed I started in '27.

Some place I musta slept out a year. An expensive sleep. A $500 sleep.

. . .

When I paid the west side fellow I asked him, "How much did it cost you for that photostat?"

"Two dollars," he said.

Five hundred for two. Say, maybe I oughta quit pitchin' and start lookin' 'round for suckers like me.

5
I'm No Satchelfoot

Now we're all square on how young I am. And how many years I been pitchin' professionally— 23. Next I want to set you right about my handle, "Satchel." 'Course you probably read about me bein' called "Satchelfoot" and "Satchmo," but both are just plain jazzed up from my original nickname when some sports writer tries to be cute.

I don't mind the "Satchmo." You know that's what they call Louie Armstrong, the trumpet man. Now I don't look like Louie and I don't act like Louie and I can't blow like Louie—except maybe with my fast ball—but Louie is a high musician favorite of mine and if "Satchmo" is good enough for him I won't decline it.

But now "Satchelfoot"—that's something different.

I don't like it, I don't want it, and I don't care who knows it.

• • •

"Satchelfoot" sounds like a clown. I ain't no clown. I ain't no end man in no Vaudeville show. I'm a baseball pitcher and winning baseball games is serious business.

• • •

Besides, my nickname's got nothing to do with my feet. I got it when I was a kid in Mobile, Alabama, where I was born. Now you know no kids have big feet, not little kids anyways, and they branded me bright and early.

All kids got nicknamed quick down in Mobile. My mother named me Leroy and she still calls me that,

16

but she's the only one. The kids named me "Satchel,"
and that's been me ever since.

Kids name each other for a reason. Like for instance we never called Eustace Wilson "Eustace." We
called him "Two Fingers" Wilson. He had 10 fingers
all right, but he never could count past the second.

I was called "Satchel" because first they saw the
satchels—then they saw me.

I was one of eleven children, the second youngest,
and my folks had little cash. Us kids had to go out and
scrape for our dimes.

Nowadays a dime seems 'bout as tiny as home plate
does to a pitcher when the umpire keeps shouting
"Ball," but in those days a dime was a load of finance.
The more you had to jingle, the richer the tune.

• • •

**I pocketed my first dime by hauling satchels in
the Mobile railroad depot. In those days there were
no fancy suitcases or contraptions like airplane lug-
gage. Travelers had plain, simple satchels.**

• • •

When the train chooed in, us kids would dash for
the satchels, grab what we could and carry them into
the depot.

I got to thinkin'. "One satchel, one dime. Two satchels, two dimes. Three satchels, three . . . the more
satchels, the more dimes." I needed more hands.

So I got me some strings, swung them 'round my
neck, shoulders and waist and tied satchels to 'em. On
a good trip I could string up sixteen satchels, put one
under each arm and two in my hands. A two dollar
pay load.

• • •

**When I was full up, the kids couldn't see me
'cause I was camouflaged like a moving satchel tree.
After that they called me "Satchel." And everybody
went looking for strings. Shoulda patented the idea.**

• • •

Later, when I was pitchin', some folks thought I was called "Satchel" 'cause when I got on the mound the victory was in the bag. I hope that's what Satch always means to the Indians.

• • •

Now you know my feet have nothing to do with my handle.

The sports writers claim my feet are anywhere from size 13s to size 16s.

They ain't. My feet are size elevens. Triple A. Maybe 'cause they're so shallow they seem so long. It's funny. When folks get the impression a fellow's got big feet, soon the feet begin to look big.

• • •

If I had big feet the kids woulda called me "Gunboats" or "Canalboats" but they didn't. They just labeled me "Satchel." Not "Satchelfoot" either.

• • •

The sports writers say I've got big feet. But I know lots of sports writers got bigger feet than me.

6
A Born Rock Thrower

We had a pretty rough gang down on the South Side of Mobile, near the Bay, where I was born and raised.

We were exclusive, that's the word. When the South Side gave a picnic, the North Side couldn't come. They always tried, for sure. But we chased them right back.

• • •

Fact is we stoned them back—with bricks. We had the best sham battlin' crew in Mobile Bay and I was known as the straightest brick thrower in Mobile.

• • •

Y' understand now, I didn't learn to be a brick thrower. It was born in me.

• • •

A musician is born with music. A pitcher is born a pitcher. He's born with his best pitch. You take this Eugene, what's his name, Bearden with the Indians. He came to his mammy with a knuckle ball. His best pitch. He was born with it.

I was born with speed and control. I came into the world with both right from the start. 'Course I didn't realize I had a gift till I began to pitch professional baseball, but I shoulda known early.

• • •

I shoulda known when I throwed my first brick.

• • •

When I throwed I didn't aim or nothin' special, but I always hit my man. Seemed like the natural thing. And I didn't question it.

If the fellow I was throwin' at hid behind a tree or a pole I'd get him anyhow, long as he left a little backside stickin' out.

And if they hid complete I'd wait 'til they did a little peekin', then wham, I got my man.

• • •

You won't believe it, but I learned my hesitation pitch throwin' bricks. If a man was throwin' at you, you wouldn't just stand there, you'd duck.

But if a man started to throw, and you ducked, and then he stopped, where would you be?

Why you'd be standin' there duckin', with your bare face, ready to be bongoed big as you please.

• • •

That's exactly how I studied out my hesitation pitch. I start my throw. The target ducks, I hesitate. He's still duckin'. Wham, I got my man.

Years later, after some of my pitchin' speed wore out I remembered that old fooler hesitation pitch.

• • •

When our South Side gang went swimmin' in the Bay we had to pass Oakdale School and the gang there wouldn't let us by, unless, of course, a cop was 'round. Some of the greatest sham battles in the history of the world took place right there by Oakdale School.

• • •

Now I know I ain't shy, and I know you ain't goin' to believe what I say right now, but this is fact: When I went swimmin' with my gang, the Oakdale School crowd didn't throw no bricks. We went by free and easy. Those Oakdale boys KNEW I was the best brick thrower in Mobile.

• • •

So did the lady truant officer. I should remember her name 'cause she came 'round to my house so often. But I don't. All I remember is we called her Mrs. Police. She would come to our homes and report "So and so is down throwin' bricks at the mules and chickens." Had to keep our arms sharp, y' understand.

But I never got in no serious trouble. Knocked a few fellows unconscious, but nothin' serious.

I know there's lotsa head knots runnin' round Mobile right now that I helped raise. When I stang those fellows then, they didn't like me nohow.

• • •

Know what they say now? They show the knot and say, nice and proud, "See this lump. Satchel grew it."

• • •

Keeps their hats from flyin' off.

7
Sniff When You Buy a Goat

I was born in a four-room house at 754 South Franklin St. in Mobile, Ala. My mother, Lulu Paige, raised 11 children in that house and she still lives there.

She's 78 now and I take care of her and my sisters. I been taking care of my mother since I been in baseball. My father died when I was knee high to him. I recollect he was a *landscraper.*

• • •

My home is in Kansas City, but my mother won't move in with me. She knows all the folks on South Franklin St. and has no hankerin' to break away. When this season is over I'm goin' down there and buy her a new home.

• • •

Four rooms can get awful crowded.

There was my sisters, Julia, Ruth, Palestine, Inez, Emma Lee, Ellen and a half-sister whose name don't seem to come to me, and my brothers, John, Wilson and Clarence, all grew up in there.

And when I was six I added a goat.

I bought the billy goat for $2.50. I got the money pickin' up some throwed-out brass and sellin' it downtown.

We built a cart for the billy and he'd haul six or seven of us at a time. We had lotsa fun with him but he smelled.

A smelly goat in a full house can make himself noticed without a single whinny-baa, believe me.

. . .

You gotta be careful in buyin' goats. Some is the smelly kind and some isn't. You can get an unsmelly one for the same price. You gotta do a little sniffin' when you buy.

. . .

Well, this goat was the smelly kind. But we became attached to him and so when Ma said "Get rid of that billy" we couldn't do it. We had a meetin' and decided to get rid of the smell instead.

We washed him every day, but never could get the odor out. Finally we figgered if we could dunk him in Mobile Bay and hold him there for a while he'd be deodorized.

It took 12 of us to carry him down to the bay. But we never did get him in.

He saw the water and he balked. We pulled and shoved and hollered and coaxed. The billy wouldn't move. We pulled so strong his horns came off. But he outstubborned the 12 of us.

. . .

We got so smelled up from the tug-o-war, we jumped in the bay. The goat turned and ran from the water fast as he could.

. . .

I know some humans the same way.

8
Rookie at Hookey

I started playin' baseball in school like most kids do. 'Course I had throwed a ball 'round the neighborhood somewhat but nothin' was really organized 'till I went to W. H. Council Grade School.

The school was kinda small but there was a field around it where lotsa baseball was played. The coach was Wilbur Hines and he lined up a team from the school and he got games with other schools. Sometimes he even got games with college teams around.

You don't have to believe it but truth is the coach played me on the Council team when I was but eight years old. When it came to baseball I always was equal to the older boys. 'Course I was always kinda tall, too, and real skinny.

• • •

And like I said about my rock throwin', I was born able to throw fast and straight. If you don't believe I came into the world with speed and control stoved in me, look at my brother Wilson. It was stoved up in him, too.

• • •

Papers have called me the fastest thrower in the world at one time or another. They ain't never seen my brother, Wilson. He was faster still. You understand now, it was something we come by at birth. Maybe my other brothers, John and Clarence coulda been pitchers too, but they never tried.

• • •

Wilson could pitch and catch and I mean PITCH

and CATCH. Everybody called him "Double Duty" Paige.

• • •

Good as Wilson was, he didn't like baseball so much. He had lotsa chances to play for money like I did but he didn't love the game. You gotta LOVE it to play it good. Me, I love it and live it.

I could pitch and catch, too, like Wilson, but they didn't call me "Double Duty" 'cause the coach hardly put me behind the plate. My fingers, he said, needed savin'.

• • •

I have told Wilson lotsa times since, if he woulda come into pro ball with me he'd be worth quarter of a million dollars today. Imagine a battery, Paige pitchin' and Paige catchin' and taking turns at each.

• • •

In grade school I played every position. Sometimes I'd begin in the outfield. If a tough batter was up Mr. Hines called me in to pitch. After I struck him out, back I'd go into the outfield, or maybe to another place. Some games I played all nine spots.

If I'd pitch the whole game I'd strike out seventeen and eighteen with nothin' but speed. I was under 10 years old strikin' out everybody.

• • •

Y' understand, if I smelled a baseball game somewhere I'd be around. Like the time a school crosstown, Emerson School, had a holiday. Was a smallpox scare there and the teachers told the kids not to come.

I knew for sure if those kids had a day off they'd be playin' ball so I talked my brother Wilson into playing hookey from our school and goin' down there to get in the game.

• • •

Somebody musta told our Ma 'cause she come a tailin' after us.

• • •

Just when we got to the ball field somebody yelled, "Here comes your Ma."

We hadda hide fast. Only thing on the field was a big pipe layin' on the ground. Wilson and I both crawled in. Ma couldn't see us but she figured we had shinnied in there. But Ma couldn't stoop down that low to look.

• • •

Wilson and I reckoned we was safe but we didn't figure on how smart our Ma was. She got some paper and rags layin' round and started a fire in one end 'o the pipe.

We was smoked out.

• • •

We come out achokin' and agaggin'.

Ma grabbed us and said, "Don't you ever play hookey again." She snatched us by the ears and marched us back home all the way crosstown. "Have you learned your lesson, boys?" she asked.

"Yes, Ma," said Wilson.

"Yes, Ma," I said.

• • •

Man, we never did play hookey again. Not after Ma burned our breeches behind us.

9
They Had to Ask My Ma

I was goin' along striking out everybody in Mobile, pitchin' for this team and that team 'round town and sometimes we'd go out o' town to beat some teams. One day we beat a good club in Luxor, Miss. and I breezed seventeen batters.

When Alex Herman heard about it he said, "That's for me."

Alex lived in Mobile, still does in fact, but he was runnin' the Chattanooga Black Lookouts in the Southern Negro League.

• • •

I was seventeen when we whopped those Luxors and Alex come 'round to see me. "How'd you like to play with the Lookouts?" he asked.

• • •

"Ask my Ma," I told him.

My Ma, y' understand, didn't like baseball, nohow. She never did see me pitch and I guess she never will. My Ma is close to the church, the Mt. Zion Baptist Church in Mobile. Fact is, my brother John is a deacon there. She thought baseball was sinnin', always playin' and never workin'.

That's why I told Alex to see her. He did. He talked and talked and talked. He told her I would get $250 a month, but he was only goin' to give me $50 of that and she would get the rest.

He showed her $200 in advance.

• • •

**She knew I couldn't make money like that no-
wheres else, so she said, "All right Mr. Herman. He's
yours for the season. But remember, I'm warning
ya, he's only a seventeen-year-old boy. You be
mother and father to him. If he comes to any harm
you'll account to me.**

"And don't miss up on those payments."

• • •

When I signed with Chattanooga in '27—I mean
'26, (now how can I mess up on that date after it
costin' me $500)—I was 6 feet 3 and a half inches tall,
same as I am now. Don't forget that half inch, lotsa
folks do. I weighed 140 pounds. If I stood sideways
you couldn't hardly notice me. Now I weigh near 180.
Gained 40 pounds in 23 years of pitchin'. If I keep it
up I'll die a fat old man.

I was throwin' the ball so hard for Chattanooga that
you couldn't see it twelve o'clock in the daytime. I'd
just tell the catchers, "Hold the mitt where you want
it. The ball will come to you." I wore out three
catcher's mitts that season. Fourteen, fifteen and more
strikeouts was average. Lotsa players were happy just
to get a foul tip.

In Chattanooga I learned I had something other
pitchers didn't have. Control! I was walkin' nobody.
When the bases got drunk, loaded y' understand, they
called me in. I realized I had a gift, throwin' the ball
where I wanted it. Up to then I thought all good
pitchers could do it.

Alex brought me back safe and sound at the end of
the season, so the next year Ma let me go out again.

Part way through '27 Alex said "Birmingham wants
you." Birmingham was in the Negro National League,
the majors to me. It meant $450 a month, $400 to Ma
and the same $50 to me.

• • •

I took it. All I was eatin' anyway those days was ice cream 'n cake and you sure could buy an awful lot o' that for $50.

• • •

Fact is, I was the sweetest man in Birmingham.

10
Did Some Boxin'

From Chattanooga to Birmingham. From Birmingham to the Nashville Elite Giants—just long enough to pick up a new Model T Ford for pocketing an important game. Back to Birmingham and points north.

I was a regular travelin' man, followin' that buck wherever it did show, jumpin' to greener pastures whenever they put out that green.

In '30 I moved up for a spell with the Cleveland Bears, playin' with fellows like Jim Willis, George William Perkins and Sam Streeter. Then over to the Baltimore Black Sox.

• • •

All the time I was aimin' at the Pittsburgh Crawfords. That was the highest of the high, the cream.

• • •

Jumpin' 'round like I was I didn't really make my mark. The country hadn't heard of me even though I was strikin' out everybody. Finally Gus Greenlee, owner of the Crawfords, got wind of my speed and he moved me onto his "Little Crawfords." I didn't play but three games with them and up I went to the varsity along with Streeter and Perkins. On that club was the great Josh Gibson, the best of the best with a bat.

With the Crawfords I got fame and a heavy load of greenbacks. The first day with the big Crawfords I was put in to throw against the Homestead Grays, that famous Smoky Joe Williams and Lefty Williams gang. I struck out sixteen using nothin' but speed.

• • •

In those days I didn't just use my fast ball constantly, I used it ALL the time.

• • •

Gus Greenlee was so happy he gave me three suits of clothes, four or five hats and signed me to a $700 a month contract. Willie Harris, a Pittsburgh politician, gave me a trophy high up to my waist.

The Crawfords was the greatest ever. We won the championship four or five times before they busted us up. If you're ever 'round Pittsburgh drop into the Crawford Grill, still owned by Gus Greenlee. He'll tell you the stories about our team you won't believe. Then he'll show you the clippin's to prove hisself.

Gus, besides ownin' the Crawfords, also owned four or five fighters, includin' John Henry Lewis, the light-heavyweight champion.

I was a crazy fool about boxin', still am, and lotsa times I'd go into Gus's gym and put the boxin' gloves on just to keep in shape. I sparred with John Henry and all the rest.

• • •

Trouble was when I stang them they'd get mad and knock me out.

• • •

One day old Gus walked in when I was layin' on the floor. He howled his choppers off and gave orders for me never to put the gloves on again.

Anyhow, in all my 23 years of playin' I never needed no boxin' skill. Closest I came was in '29 with Birmingham. We were playin' the St. Louis Stars for the second half title and leadin' by three games. Bill

Gatewood, he lives in Moberly, Missouri now, was managin' our club.

• • •

"Satch," he said, "I want you to pitch close to the handle to those boys. Dust 'em off."

I did exactly, and busted the first three batters' thumbs.

• • •

Candy Jim Taylor (he died not long ago) was managin' the Stars. He rushed out and told Gatewood, "If Satch keeps pitchin' we're quittin'."

"Then quit," said Gatewood, "'cause Satch is pitchin'."

The Stars started packin' up, but one of their players, Henry Murray, was too mad to leave. He picked up a bat and started chasin' me.

• • •

When I got near second base he let fly. I dodged and the bat whizzed past. I picked it up and did my own chasin'.

• • •

Murray left in a hurry.

Satchel Paige (Photos from the collection of John B. Holway).

Paige pitching in Puerto Rico (Courtesy of Luis Alvelo).

With the monarchs.

Paige's high-step pitching style.

The 1933 Pittsburgh Crawfords line up: Paige, Leroy Matlock, W. Bell, Harry Kincannon, Sam Streeter, and Bertram Hunter.

Paige (far right) with 1942 Kansas City Monarchs pitching staff. Others pictured, from left, Hilton Smith, Jack Matchett, Booker McDaniels, Jim LaMarque and Connie Johnson.

With Bill Veeck.

Paige with Tom Baird (left), owner of the Kansas City Monarchs, and Lefty Gomez.

With Dizzy Dean.

Paige with his teammate, Jackie Robinson, on the Kansas City Monarchs, 1945.

Paige with longtime friend and batting star, Josh Gibson.

11
Travelin' Man

More people has seen me pitch than any other pitcher ever lived. That's 'cause I pitched more and everywhere. I been in every state in the United States except Maine and Boston.

Excuse me, I made Boston with the Indians.

This is my twenty-third year of pitchin' and when I say YEAR I mean 365 days. I been pitching 130 to 160 games a season regular, and only 'til recent did I stop pitchin' whole games.

I been told they called old Ed Walsh the Iron Man 'cause he throwed 56 games one year. That ought to make me some kinda Man o' Distinction.

• • •

I figure I have pitched over 2,000 games, travelin' near 30,000 miles a year. Springs down South. Summers in the U.S. Falls in California and winters in Latin and South America.

• • •

The most I ever struck out in any one game was 18 or 19, maybe 20. I don't remember which, but whichever it was I did it lotsa times.

I have pitched so many no-hit games I disremember the number. But you can bet as high as you please, nobody else come near it. 'Cause I had more chances.

I have got all kindsa gifts for my throwin'. I got automobiles, suits, hundreds of gold watches, near a thousand hats, and truckloads of lovin' cups. The cups I give away to YMCAs.

• • •

The cash I kept. Most I ever got for one night's pitchin' was $2,800 against Dizzy Dean's team in Washington during the war. My standard rate when I was booked through the Kansas City Monarchs from 1940 on was $500 for three innins'.

• • •

Most I ever made in one season was $35,000. "Believe It or Not" Ripley said it was $40,000. Don't believe it.

• • •

I'm glad the income tax folks didn't take Believe it or Not's word as gospel.

• • •

I have played on over a hundred teams. Sometimes I was playin' with 10 teams at once. Like, for instance, folks ask me, "Where were you pitchin' in '33?"
"The Crawfords."
"But I thought you was pitchin' with . . ."
"Well I was."
But I seen you pitchin' with . . ."
"Well I did."

• • •

The Crawfords booked me around. So did the Monarchs later. On different nights the same week I'd be with Memphis, the Monarchs, the Homestead Grays and the House of David.

• • •

I was the only player on the Davids without a beard. 'Course I had a mustache. Had it when I came to the Indians.
When I signed with Cleveland I said to Mr. Bill Veeck, "What about the mustache?"
"What about it?" he asked.

"I got one," I said.

"So I see," he said.

"Should I keep it?" I asked.

"It's yours to keep or cut," he told me. "But nobody else in the majors has one."

• • •

Neither have I.

12
Duel with Josh

The first major league player I ever faced was Hack Wilson of the Chicago Cubs. I struck him out. Babe Herman followed him. I struck Babe out, too.

That was in 1930. There was another Babe on that team, by the name of Ruth. It was his ball club. I was with the Baltimore Black Sox and we was barnstormin' together.

• • •

But I never got to pitch to Mr. Ruth. When I was pitchin' he wasn't playin' and when he was playin' I wasn't pitchin'. A keen regret I have is I never pitched to Mr. Ruth.

• • •

I did throw against all the rest, though. When Paul and Lloyd Waner was hittin' fools for the Pittsburgh Pirates I throwed against them plenty on the Coast. Never had no trouble. Only one major league hitter ever did trouble me. He was Charlie Gehringer, second baseman for the Detroit Tigers. Ken Keltner of the Indians bothered me some when I barnstormed against Bob "Rapid" Feller's team, but not as often as Gehringer.

Gehringer stood up at that plate flatfooted. You couldn't fool him. 'Course he got nothin' but singles. But singles can be bothersome. Lots of times I'd walk Charlie to get at the next batter.

I'd rather face a Waner or a DiMaggio or a Williams than a Gehringer.

• • •

But the best of all was Josh Gibson.

• • •

Josh was my catcher with the Pittsburgh Crawfords. The advertising would say: "The Greatest Battery in Baseball—Josh Gibson, guaranteed to knock two home runs, and Satchel Paige, guaranteed to strike out the first nine men." Both of us would do it, too.

When Gibson was traded to the Homestead Grays I hated to pitch to him.

Josh hit homers in every major league park we played. He hit the farthest balls I ever saw. When the Crawfords sold him to the Homestead Grays he hit me, too. Singles, no homers, but he hit me.

I could throw the ball at him and he would look like I fooled him perfect. Next, I looked, the ball was sailing over my head into the outfield.

• • •

Josh was built like Joe Louis and could punch like Joe Louis. Only with a bat. If Josh was livin' today the major league teams would be cuttin' hogs to get him.

• • •

About 1932 we both went to Puerto Rico to play durin' the winter. After a game one day we headed for the beach. We was all layin' in the sun and Josh and me had a kinda argument 'bout if he was a better batter than I was a pitcher.

• • •

Josh said, "Satch, some day my whole family is goin' to be in the stands and all your friends, too, includin' Gus Greenlee and Willie Harris of Pittsburgh. You'll be pitchin' and I'll come up with the bases filled. Know what I'm going to do? I'm goin' to drive you and the ball clear out to left field."

• • •

Everybody laughed and I grinned. I said, "We'll see."

Well, it happened in 1942. I was pitchin' with the Kansas City Monarchs and Josh was with the Homesteads and we was playin' in Pittsburgh in a two-out-of-three playoff series. The score was 6–3, two outs, last of the eighth.

Gus Greenlee was in the stands and Willie Harris. Josh's whole family was watchin'.

The first batter, Judge Wilson, got a single. Easterland and Buck Leonard was comin' up next.

I called "time" and walked up to my catcher, Frank Duncan, who was also managin' our team. "Frank," I said, "I'm goin' to walk Easterland and Buck-Leonard."

He looked at me like I was drunk. "That's goin' to bring up Josh Gibson," he said.

• • •

"Exactly right. That's why I want to do it," and I told him why. "It will be a great thrill for me. You know I been in baseball a long time and this is my moment."

"Okay," Duncan said, "Go ahead."

• • •

I walked Easterland on purpose. My whole team run in at me. The owner of the club, John Wilkinson, come out on the field. They all was popeyed. But I explained them back to normal.

I walked Buck Leonard fillin' the bases and up come Josh Gibson swingin' his big bat. I told all my infielders and outfielders to camp out in left field where Josh promised to ride the ball.

• • •

The stands had been howlin' but now they buzzed a bit and turned dead quiet.

• • •

I yelled to Josh. "Remember Puerto Rico? Well the bases is filled.

"Now you're too smart to fool, so I'm goin' to tell you what's comin'. I'm goin' to throw you two sidearm fast balls down around the knees." The umpire was John Craig, I remember clear.

Josh let the first pitch go.

Craig called, "Strike one."

Josh let the second pitch go.

Craig called, "Strike two."

"Now," I said, "Josh, you're too good for me to waste any pitches so I'm goin' to finish you with a sidearm curve. That's your weakness."

I threw it and Josh stepped back. It broke over and he swung a slow motion strike three.

• • •

Josh come out to the box and shook my hand.

They had to halt play for 'bout an hour to clear the field of straw hats.

13
Bonuses in Bismarck

In 1933 a fellow in Bismarck, N.D., cried "Help" and I came a runnin'. The man's name was Neil Churchill, the mayor of the town and the man they wanted to put in Congress 'til he said no.

How the "Help" call came about was another town in North Dakota—Jamestown—had brought in a colored battery for their team, the Hancock Brothers and another colored thrower, a good one too, Barney Brown.

The Hancocks and Brown made the Jamestowns great stuff and the folks there began givin' Bismarck the hee-haw.

Mr. Churchill took the jibes personal-like and he told the Jamestown folks, "Just you watch, I'll round up a team to beat you."

They laughed but they didn't know Mr. Churchill. If you laugh at him you don't laugh twice.

• • •

He wrote a letter to Abe Saperstein, who was helpin' Negro baseball promote their leagues. "Who," he asked, "is the best Negro pitcher in baseball?"

Mr. Saperstein wrote, "Satchel Paige of the Pittsburgh Crawfords."

• • •

That's all Mr. Churchill needed. He got me. He made a deal with the Crawfords so I could pitch for both teams. He give me $300 a month and expenses and a house to live in free. Besides I was supposed to play with the Crawfords when they needed me, which was often, and they was to pay me too. I didn't do so bad figurin' it was kind of a depression.

The day I come to Bismarck we was playin' Jamestown. They scored a run in the third inning and I said to Mr. Churchill, "They will score no more runs." They didn't, naturally, and Mr. Churchill gave me a BONUS. After that everytime I won, which was always, he gave me some kinda bonus.

I pitched for the Bismarks through '35. Mr. Churchill began expandin', playin' the major leaguers comin' through and the best colored teams. We made some barnstormin' trips up to Canada, too. Mr. Churchill signed up Quincy Troupe, who is now managin' and catchin' for the Chicago American Giants, Red Haley, a Cuban first baseman, and Barney Morris and Hilton Smith, two good colored pitchers. The rest of the team was white. We had a Jewish second baseman, a Lithuanian shortstop, an Italian third baseman, a Swede center fielder, a German in right, and an Irishman in left.

At the beginnin' of '35 Mr. Churchill gave me a brand new Chrysler automobile, with all the trimmins'. There was mud guards on each wheel and they had lights which lit up, blinkin' on and off. The horns was loud and long and could play tunes. I could spotlight up that car like a circus wagon. And I did.

• • •

Mr. Churchill, y'understand, owned the Chrysler agency in town. One day I seen a rear-view mirror with a clock on it in his showroom. I was missin' one and I said to Mr. Churchill, "How about this?"

"It's yours," he said, "if you win tonight's game."

"I'm windin' up right now," I told him. I knew that shiny tick-tock was mine.

• • •

When we was playin' an exhibition in Canada against Earl Mack's All-Stars before they left for Japan, I seen Mr. Churchill with a sleek .22 rifle. I had a hankerin' for it. "Beat them tonight and it's yours," he said.

They had big league hitters like Heinie Manush, Jimmy Foxx and Earl Averill.

I whopped them 10-0 for that shooter.

One day the St. Paul team come through town after winnin' the American Association championship. They had been knockin' everybody off real good.

The first batter was Lou Fette, who went up to the Boston Braves. My openin' pitch came close to his head. He yelled, "You so and so, I'll come out and knock your brains out."

I told him, "You better stay where you are, you'll have plenty to do." The first eight men struck out. Only hit they got was on an infield fly I tried to catch behind my back for show.

• • •

We won 96 out of 104 games that year. And I pitched in near every one. Remember I was pitchin' for the Crawfords too. We could have won them all, but some of the opposin' managers asked Mr. Churchill for a break. Like for example after we won the Denver Post tournament we was playin' an exhibition series against the House of David. Ray Doan, the promoter, asked Mr. Churchill to let the Davids win one game to keep the series interestin'. So he pitched the 16-year-old batboy.

• • •

One time a stranger in McPherson, Kan., made fun of our town. He said to Mr. Churchill, "You mean that two-bit Bismarck, SOUTH DAKOTA, got a team?"

"We're from NORTH DAKOTA," said Mr. Churchill, "and I'll bet you anything you wish on tonight's game."

The man bet $300.

After we was winnin' 13-0 in the fifth innin', Mr. Churchill called in our infield and outfield leavin' just me and my catcher. They ain't nobody on that McPherson team reached first yet.

From McPherson we moved into Wichita for the big tournament run by Ray Dumont. The best semi-pro teams from all over the country loaded up and came to that.

Mr. Churchill said if we won that tournament he would give me another automobile. Our toughest game was our first game. Word got 'round that the pitcher on the other club was out to beanball me.

• • •

But he was up at bat first and I tickled his ribs. He wasn't smilin' when they carried him off. We won the tournament.

• • •

Then we went down to Kansas City to play the Monarchs who had just grabbed the Negro world series. Our boys was hurt and we had only 10 men in uniform. They stole 11 bases on our catcher and I was feelin' sad. They was winnin', 3-1. I wasn't gettin' no corners from the umpire and I told Mr. Churchill I wanted to come out.

"Satch," he said, "this is my last game as a baseball manager. I'm through after this one. I want you to stay in and win it for me. You're supposed to go and barnstorm with Dizzy and Paul Dean after tonight. How much are they givin' you?"

"Three seventy-five for a month's tour."

"I'll give you $750 if we win this game."

We won, 8–3.

• • •

I will always do anything I can for Mr. Churchill. This year he went back to baseball for the first time.

Fact is, I was headin' back to Bismarck to help him when the pennant burnin' Indians smoked me out.

• • •

That's one fire I hope ain't never unlit.

14
Snakes and Guns

'Bout the end of the 1936 season Gus Greenlee was havin' a little financial bout with the depression and his Pittsburgh Crawfords ball club began breakin' up.

The story is I was sold to the Newark Eagles to pay off a debt. Gus says this ain't true and I never did see no contract, so when folks say I jumped away from Newark ask them to show you the contract.

• • •

Where I did jump to was South America. Some big sugar plantation man named Pete Something gimme a call. The sugar man says he put $2,800 in a U.S. bank under my name and there is $500 a week, room and board free, awaitin' in Valencia, Venezuela if I'll come down and pitch for his team.

• • •

I came a runnin' with five other players. He had three natives on his ball club and we was usin' rules datin' way back to 1907. The umpires was picked right out of the sugar fields and ain't never see a ball game before. The natives come to the games in crowds but they didn't know what was goin' on. They just come. But Pete Something, he paid us the money.

I had been south of the border before. Ever since '29 I'd been goin' to Puerto Rico to play in the winter leagues. But Puerto Rico wasn't nothin' like Venezuela. In Puerto Rico baseball was serious.

• • •

Once when I was pitchin' for Guayama, Puerto

Rico, I won 24 straight games. All by myself. I lose the
next one, 1–0, and the whole town stops speakin' to
me. They accused me of layin' down. They said I
musta been drunk.

In Venezuela it was opposite. Pete Something was
serious enough, but hardly anybody knew the game
'cept us Americans. I did the teachin'. But Peter was
happy 'cause we kept winnin'. For winnin' a big game
once he took five of us in a bird to Hamburg, Ger-
many on a little vacation. I didn't like it too thorough
there 'cause that was when old Hitler was beginnin' to
break through his wall paper.

· · ·

**I coulda made a fortune in Venezuela without
pitchin' a ball but I was sleepin' standin' up. One
day I see a bow-legged jackass. "I said to myself,
that's a cute jackass." When I come back to the States
there's that old jackass standin' round on his bow
legs in a side-show pullin' in the dollars.**

· · ·

When I wasn't pitchin' down there I played the
outfield so the team could take advantage of my hittin'. I don't mind announcin' I can hit, and I told Mr.
Boudreau I'm always ready with the stick. I never
batted less than .300 any season.

One time in Caracas, Venezuela I was playin' the
outfield and I seen an iron pipe on the ground. I paid
it no more attention. In the fifth innin', a fly ball
comes out my way, rolls up to the pipe and stops.
Then the pipe begins movin'. I moved too. Right for
the clubhouse.

· · ·

**That pipe was a snake. Looked like a boa con-
strictor. The batter got a home run, 'cause for all I
know the ball is still layin' out there.**

I never did play the outfield again.

• • •

One winter a man by the name of Dr. Jose Enrique Aybar money-talked most of us Pittsburgh Crawford players into goin' down to San Domingo to play for a town named Cuidad Trujillo.

The town was named after the president of San Domingo, Di Rafael L. Trujillo. He was the boss of everything and we was his team.

Dr. Aybar was the manager and when he got us down there he said, "Boys! Here's some advice. You'd better win."

"What do you mean?" I asked.

He didn't have to answer. I see a soldier standin' by tuggin' at a gun. From then on all I could see was Trujillo's soldiers tuggin' at guns.

We was his team y'understand and we was supposed to advertise he was a winner by winnin' ourselves. Politics, y'understand.

• • •

If we went swimmin' the soldiers with guns were chaperones. We had soldiers on our hotel floors, too. Trujillo gave orders anyone in town sellin' us whiskey would be shot.

I didn't mind the soldiers. But the guns was gettin' me jittery.

• • •

Then Trujillo cooks up a series with a team called Estrellas de Oriente. Who do you think was runnin' that team but the man who was tryin' to beat Trujillo out for the presidentship! See the politics they was playin'? It was like the election depended on the series. The Estrellas wasn't no easy pickin'. They was loaded with American players, too.

We was jittery and we lost three out of the first six games. The final—and main game—was played in Trujillo's town. Seven thousand people was in the stands and they all have knives and guns.

I tried to play sick. 'Cause I was sick, believe me. But they stuck a gun at my head and I got well.

. . .

The umpires was Trujillo's men, too. I knowed if I throwed the ball anywhere it would be a strike 'cause the umpires saw the guns too, but I was shakin' like a leaf in a high breeze and they had us 5–4 goin' into the seventh. We got two runs that innin' and I said to myself, "L-l-l-listen S-s-s-atch," (I couldn't talk to myself without stutterin') "pull yourself together before they air-condition you."

. . .

Well we lucked through the next two innins' and won, 6–5.

The American consul heard what a worrysome situation we was in and they flew us out in a bird that same night.

Later in the States I was readin' a statement from Dr. Aybar that baseball in Trujillo City ain't commercial. "Money makes no difference," he said. "Baseball is spiritual in every respect as indulged in by the Latin races."

. . .

Them guns wasn't spiritual. But they near made a spirit outa me.

15
Curves in Mexico

I was havin' a little food trouble (I'm gonna tell you about that later) in Venezuela in '38 so I moved up north to Mexico and that move nearly finished me.

I was pitchin' for Mexico City in the Mexican League. My sufferin' stomach kinda sapped some of the strength from my arm, so I figured the time has come for me to start savin' speed and throwin' curves. 'Til then I used nothin' but blindin' speed. No windup, nothin'. Just rear back and throw it fast.

I seen the other fellows breakin' the ball so I decided my time has come. I started tryin' to break curves.

Now let me give you some advice. If you is hankerin' to be a pitcher don't start your curve balls in Mexico. A curve ball is throwed with spin. And the spin does somethin' to the air which makes the air get mad at the ball and push it away and that's a curve.

• • •

But in Mexico City, y' understand, there ain't so much air 'cause it's up so high. If there is less air, less can get mad and it don't shove on the ball much so it don't curve much.

• • •

I worked harder 'n harder tryin' to angry up the air but my arm got mad instead.

It ached all over and I couldn't hardly throw.

The club owners thought I was loafin' 'cause I began to use only foolin' slow stuff. I got by the batters, winnin' five out of seven, but the owners wanted speed so they sent me home.

My arm ached so bad I couldn't scratch my head.
In a way I was worried. Now I would have to find me
a workin' job.

• • •

**But I was saved from that by Mr. John Wilkinson
who owned the Kansas City Monarchs.**

• • •

Mr. Wilkinson said he'd pay me $1,000 a month to
travel with the Monarchs as a coach. All I had to do
was stand in the first base coaching box durin' the
game and put on a pepper show before the game. A
"pepper show" means doin' tricks with the ball like
makin' it roll all around your body like it was on
strings and tricks like that. I ain't done it in the majors
'cause I ain't seen anybody else do it. Maybe they
can't.

I always had trouble with calendars 'n clocks so Mr.
Wilkinson bought me a bird and had his son fly me
'round in it. That way I always got to places on time.
They say I am like Rube Waddell, not showin' up for
games and such, but I show up when I know about
them. Like in New York last July. I didn't come to
Yankee Stadium one afternoon 'cause it was rainin'
and anyway I thought it was a night game.

• • •

**Mr. Boudreau fined me $100. Fifty for missin' the
game and fifty for missin' the train to Boston that
night. And he gave me a baseball schedule, too. That
$100 guaranteed I would keep lookin' at it.**

• • •

Well, with the Monarchs I did no throwin' at all, not
even a coupla feet. I was so disgusted with myself that
I didn't even play catch. Nobody was gonna see a
shadow of the old me. I was finished, washed up and I
wanted to forget I ever throwed.

One hot day we were playin' an exhibition in Winnipeg, Canada. I was standin' in the first base coachin' box when a ball come toward me from the bullpen. Not thinkin' I picked it up and threw it back.

• • •

'Bout two minutes went by and my brain all of a sudden asks me, "How did the ball get back in the bullpen?"

"I throwed it," I answers.

"Maybe your arm is comin' 'round," my brain says.

"Maybe it is," I replies.

• • •

I walked down to the bullpen and started warmin' up.

All the Monarchs stopped play and come around to watch. "It comin' 'round Satch, it's comin' 'round," they said like they seen a miracle.

Three days later Mr. Wilkinson put me in for two innings. I struck out all six batters. "That's enough for today, Satch," he said.

• • •

I been in my second childhood ever since.

16
Telling the World

Well my arm was back but now the problem was to let folks know about it. Mr. John Wilkinson decided the best man to do that was Abe Saperstein, the owner of the world famous Harlem Globetrotters Negro basketball team and the man who helped build up the East-West Negro All-Star Baseball Game.

Mr. Wilkinson took me up to see Abe. Abe's got his office on 192 North Clark Street in Chicago.

Mr. Wilkinson said to Abe, "Satch's arm has come around. That means he's probably the world's greatest pitcher again, but we got to let the fans know about it. You're just the man for the job."

Abe said he'd see what he could do. And they made a deal. The deal was Abe was to get first call on my services. Somethin' like the deal Joe Louis' managers had with Mike Jacobs.

Well, Abe and Mr. Wilkinson started plottin'.

Abe says, "If Satch is great again let's let his arm speak for us. The hottest pitcher in Negro baseball is Roosevelt Davis. How about putting Satch up against him?"

I says, "Now wait. That Roosevelt Davis throws a cut ball. I don't like to throw no cut ball. I ain't used to it."

"What's a cut ball?" asks Abe.

Mr. Wilkinson told him, "A cut ball is a ball that has cuts in it. Davis scratches the ball with his nails and his belt buckle. That makes the ball sail and Davis knows how to control it."

• • •

Abe says, "Well Satch. It looks like you'll have to throw a cut ball whether you want to or not."

"If I gotta, I gotta," I says.

• • •

So Abe books a game late in September with the Palmer House Indians, the team Roosevelt Davis was pitchin' for. The Palmer House Indians was made up of colored stars who spent their off-season workin' 'round the Palmer House Hotel in Chicago. The team had a long winnin' streak and everybody was beginnin' to think nobody could beat 'em.

Abe booked the game for the Chicago White Sox ball park.

"Now," he says, "we've got to work on the newspapers." He took me to the Chicago *Daily News* to see his friend Lloyd Lewis. Mr. Lewis at that time was combined sports editor and dramatic critic for the paper. Mr. Lewis talked to me 'bout an hour and he wrote two stories about me. Those stories are now in a book called *It Takes All Kinds*.

Man, those stories did it. That White Sox park was filled to the top seat. I told Mr. Wilkinson, "Cut ball or no cut ball, we gotta win. I'll tell you what to do. You stand on the dugout steps and hold up your fingers so I can see. Every time a man goes out hold up a finger. That way I'll know how many outs. Sometimes I forget."

Mr. Wilkinson did. I struck out the first four men. Just to give the rest of the Palmer House boys the idea, y'understand, Mr. Wilkinson kept showin' me the outs and I kept makin' 'em. They got three hits and we win, 1-0.

• • •

But I still don't like no cut ball. Hasn't got a smooth feel.

• • •

After the game Abe called up Mr. Lewis for advice. "What do you think should be our next move?"

Mr. Lewis says, "Let's show Satch to New York. I've got some good friends there who can help."

Know who his friends were? Kaufman and Hart. That's right George Kaufman and Moss Hart, the fellows who wrote all kindsa stage plays like *The Man Who Came to Dinner.* I don't know if the man ever did eat that meal but I do know Kaufman and Hart been eatin' pretty good from it.

Well, those two fellows fixed it for me. I got good notices in the papers and when we played the New York Cubans in Yankee Stadium the crowd was heavy. After I throwed another shutout there the fans knew my arm was back.

• • •

So did the batters.

17
A Bag of Tricks

When the miracle was passed in 1939 and my arm come 'round to normal, a little somethin' was left out. I didn't have all my blindin' speed, just blazin' speed, and I couldn't throw fast constantly or even all the time like before. I had to save my blazer for spots.

I seen the time had come for me to be cute. The batters had to be outthunk. So I began to cute up. I taught myself to throw three ways, sidearm, overhand and underhand. I conjured up a curve three ways. Y'understand now, an underhand curve is a rare ball. But I got it. Ain't throwed it in the majors yet but when I do some batter's peepers is gonna pop. Lotsa balls I ain't showed in the majors yet.

• • •

Things has been so serious with the Indians. I ain't hankerin' to cause no laughs and when I get extra cute sometimes even I gotta smile.

• • •

I got all kindsa windups rangin' from no windup to my windmill wheel in which my arms keep whirlin' 'til I tell 'em to stop. The special windups is to throw the batters off stride.

I fascinates them with my arms and they forget a ball is gonna be throwed. Same reason for both my hesitation windup and my hesitation pitch which sprang back from my rock throwin' days. The hesitation pitch is the one folks call "Stepin Pitchit." I don't care what name they do give it long as the batters don't Stepin Hitit. And they don't.

• • •

I got bloopers, loopers and droopers. I got a jump ball, a be ball, a screw ball, a wobbly ball, a whipsy-dipsy-do, a hurry-up ball, a nothin' ball and a bat dodger.

• • •

My be ball is a be ball 'cause it "be" right where I want it, high and inside. It wiggles like a worm.

Some I throw with my knuckles, some with two fingers. My whipsy-dipsy-do is a special fork ball I throw underhand and sidearm that slithers and sinks. I keep my thumb off the ball and use three fingers. The middle finger sticks up high, like a bent fork.

But the main thing is, I got control. When I was with the Monarchs and the House of Davids I did stunts for the folks before the game. I throwed balls between two bats standin' up at home plate six inches apart. I knocked cigars out of batters' mouths.

• • •

Watch me when I warm up. I don't pitch for home plate. I stick a small match box or a tiny piece of cigaret paper in front of the catcher instead. I figure if I can throw over a small target like a match box I sure can get it over a great big plate.

• • •

Now I ain't braggin' 'bout my control. It ain't my fault I have it. I was born with it. But the pitches, I brung them into the world myself. They's original with me, and I been 'speriencin' with some secret ones. They's all legal, too.

Some of the umpires been talkin' about rulin' out my hesitation windup with a man on third. In the first place I don't use it with a man on third. In the second place it's legal if I does. They think I'm hesitatin' but I really ain't. They think I'm stoppin' still. But I ain't. Some part of me is movin' all the time.

They can call it a balk if they want. But it ain't.

Accordin' to the rules a balk is a pitch that fools a base runner. If I take a windup I can't throw to a base. That's the rules. So if I take a hesitation windup, the runner knows I can't throw to pick him off. I ain't foolin' him. I'm foolin' the batter.

• • •

Ain't that what a pitcher's supposed to do?

18
Dave Writes Me Up

One of my best friends was Dave Hawkins, a colored writer who often had his stuff printed in the best papers and magazines in the nation. Dave died of TB a few years back, but while he was living he used to send me letters all over the country.

Now I ain't very good at answerin' my mail 'cause I'm always on the move but I enjoyed Dave's letters so much I would store them up and answer him a big long one—from Mexico or Canada or wherever I was.

Dave also managed a fighter, Wilson Hurry-Up Yarbo, and for laughs there was nothin' like watchin' Yarbo. Yarbo was somethin' like me. He'd take a long windmill windup with his left hand, and while his opponent got hypnotized watchin' he'd sneak in that right sucker punch.

• • •

Yarbo could stand in the center of the ring, and weave his body without movin' his legs so he'd dodge most of the punches the other fellow was throwin'. Yarbo got laughs but he didn't get no titles 'cause every now and then he forgot to dodge.

• • •

But gettin' back to Dave Hawkins. He once covered a game I pitched in Cleveland's League Park. That's where the Indians used to play before the crowds got so big League Park got too small and the team moved into the Stadium. Well this game that Dave Hawkins covered was between the Kansas City Monarchs and the St. Louis Stars. It was a regular Negro American League game. I was pitchin' for the Monarchs and

Hilton Smith throwed for the Stars. The date was in August of 1941.

That Dave Hawkins could really write words. I always saved the story and here it is:

Next to Mistah Joseph Barrow (Joe Louis to you), that Alabama Flame-Throwing Leroy Satchel Paige is the greatest draw in all Coal Grove (that's Harlem anywheres).

Like my Aunt Lucy's corset string he is indeed some pull and yesterday he pulled them into League Park like a new mud pack at the beauty parlor. Number kings to commoners were all there like amens at prayer meeting to gawk at brother Leroy do his stipulated stint of five innings on the League Park causeway.

It saddens the heart of your agent here like having to eat a pet hog to have to adominish a few of my beloved brothers who came away intimating that some of the octane had evaporated out of Parson Paige's petrol.

• • •

Those skeptical guntmans got that way just because old Satch's whammeroo ball that usually comes up there no bigger'n an aspirin tablet was shelved for the day. I remit that the one he was oozing up there looked bigger'n a Georgia watermelon, but it sho wasn't no strip tease 'cause it had plenty on it.

• • •

Furthermore some of the infielders who have come close to getting arrested for loitering while Mr. Paige was striking all the batters out, were begging the human hair pin yesterday to let them throw out a few so the boss could see they were still worthy of their hire.

So to give some of the infield a chance to show off, the great Mose mound artist laid away his "hurry-up ball" and profusely applied his new "bat dodger," deftly putting it in just the right places where it would decompose the highest hopes and keep a whole passel of boys swinging like a bunch of epileptic trap drummers. Proving, indeed, the good smart Parson Paige might be getting a little bald but it ain't showing on the inside.

Moping up and down the mound like Stepin Fetchit bogged down, the Satch confided that the crowd wouldn't see much of his "hurry-up" ball, too, on accounta underground word had leaked to him that Manager George Mitchell of the St. Louis Stars had instructed his lads that the good Dr. Paige didn't have nuthing but an armful of wham and to just lay back and cut it, so he was going to show them that the new "bat dodger" which indeed did soon have a lot of the boys suffering a mess of optical indigestion.

So with Satch up there keeping the lustily swinging St. Louis Stars grounding all around, that zippy Kansas City Monarch infield was making more double plays than a crooked wife.

•   •   •

Guess the score was unimportant 'cause Dave Hawkins never mentioned it.

19
Stick with Feller

I been pitchin' against major leaguers ever since 1930. Autumns we went barnstormin' together. Babe Ruth had a team, Earl Mack had a team. Dizzy Dean had a team. Lefty Goofy Gomez had a team. Bobo Newsom had a team. Bob Rapid Feller had a team. I ain't gonna brag how I did. Ask Bob Rapid.

Now I'm gonna speak right up for Bob Rapid. First time I seen him was in 1936. I throwed against him in an exhibition game in Des Moines, Iowa after he finished his first season with Cleveland. The lights was bad and we both was strikin' out everybody. The batter was swingin' in self protection. I winned that game by one run. But man, that boy was fast.

• • •

He still is fast, too, He had a little trouble with control this season. But he's comin' out of it.

• • •

Now after I had my arm trouble in '38 I had to cute up. Bob Rapid is cutin' up right now, but he don't have to cute up so much 'cause he still got speed. Maybe not as much as before, but more than most. When the old control comes 'round Bob Rapid is gonna rack up those ball games as fast as I get tickets for speedin'. And that ain't seldom.

• • •

I know exactly how Bob Rapid felt inside when the folks booed him for missin' the 1948 All-Star game. It wasn't his fault but you can't go out on the field with a sign on your back sayin' "Folks, you're

all wrong. Listen to my story." You're convicted and there's no repeal.

Same thing happened to me in 1944.

• • •

Each year we have a Negro All-Star game in Comiskey Park, Chicago. In '44 the fans, as always, voted me to pitch and I was proud. It was durin' the war and I told the club owners the money should go to the GI's. They said, "No." So I said, "I ain't pitchin'."

They passed the word along that I was walkin' out 'cause I wanted a bigger cut. But I outstubborned them and didn't play. Next time I was pitchin' was in Philadelphia and when they announced my name I was booed, same as Bob Rapid.

But home plate wasn't booin' so I got along all right and soon word got around that I was holdin' out for the GI's and the booin' stopped.

Bob Rapid's trouble I reckon was his bein' over-anxious to make good. He's straightenin' 'round. But there's only one way. He hadda keep pitchin'. When Bob Rapid was losin' I heard folks say Mr. Boudreau should drop him as a starter. Why man, you can't do that. You can't stove up on your leader and Bob Rapid is our leader.

• • •

If he is right there wouldn't be no pennant race. He'd lead us right to the promised land. Cleveland gotta stick with him so he can stay right.

• • •

Durin' the '48 season Bob had a little trouble with Joe DiMaggio. You won't believe me but I would walk a man anytime to get to Joe DiMaggio. I'd bet the world and a ball of fire that Joe don't do no damage against me nohow. He's goin' to wait for his pitch. And I ain't going to give it to him.

The batters that bother me are the weak ones. They can't swing near as good as Joe but they ain't choosy. They swing at anything and poke a fluke.

I struck out Joe in Yankee Stadium with a curve ball breakin' away. But I was doggone sure the ball was breakin' WAY away.

• • •

Also you gotta remember this. Don't throw Joe no slow stuff. And keep it away from his belt. High and inside—my "Be ball"—is safe.

• • •

And be careful when you pitch to Ted. Ted Williams, y'understand. I struck him out, too, in Boston. Only the umpire called it a ball. Ted knowed he was struck out. The umpire was struck out, too. He said so later, hisself.

They told me Ted was smart. The count was three and two on him and I asked myself, "What is Ted thinkin'?"

He's thinkin' "That old man's got control and he's goin' for a corner." So I give him my nothin' ball. Nothin' on it, straight over the center. I outcuted him that time. But I wouldn't try it again. Not on Ted.

When I'm pitchin' I walk the rubber. Never pitch from the same spot twice. Move up and down and feel the batter. Somethin' like that radar. A bull-fighter watches the bull's knees. Long as he watches the knees he ain't gonna get hurt. I do the same with the batters. Only trouble, some of them wears fooling pants down to the ankles. Like Mickey Vernon of Washington. I feeled him out with a "Be ball." That droved him away from the plate. While he's away I throwed my whipsy-dipsy-do over the outside corner. "Strike Three."

• • •

Lots of times I waste pitches to set up pitches. When I got three-and-two on a batter, I ain't in the hole. The batter is. He knows the next one is gonna get a piece of the plate and he's gotta swing.

. . .

I done some extra special figurin' for night games. When I was with the Monarchs we carried our own lights and poles. I was one of the first pitchers that throwed at night. When the sun is shinin' the light bounces 'round and brightens all sides. But the night game lamps shine only straight down. They light up only the top of a baseball. The bottom is dark. I throws 'em low at night. That shows the batter less top. The less top I shows the less is lit. The less is lit the less he sees. The less he sees, the less he hits. If at all.

. . .

Even with my trick pitches my main strikeout ball still is my fast ball. It's lots faster than folks think it is.

. . .

And it don't hurt a pitcher to be a little superstitious. I got a couple pet ones. I always wear two pairs of stockins'. I'm kinda superstitious that if a ball hits my shins it's gonna hurt. A little extra paddin' ain't temptin' fate.

I always put on my left shoe first and tie it. First time I did I throwed a great game so I kept doin' it.

Another superstition is after each innin' I take my glove into the dugout. Nobody else in the majors does it. Mr. Boudreau says it's all right for me to leave the glove on the field. So now I do.

. . .

Nobody stole it yet.

20
Hobbies Keep Me Young

My idea of livin' is you gotta keep movin'. You gotta have lotsa things to do and you gotta do them good. You gotta keep movin' and you gotta keep thinkin'. That's why I been able to go so long.

I love baseball and keep thinkin' about it most of the day, when I'm takin' my two hot baths and even when I'm tyin' my shoes. But I do lotsa other things in a kinda relaxin' way.

Like I'm crazy 'bout Spanish music. I'm always playin' and makin' records in my hotel room. I like rhumbas, congas, boleros but the best is calypso music. I can sing the doggonest calypso songs. Got my own guitar, too. A four-string tenor guitar for my own amusement, y'understand. Y'oughta hear some of my calypso records. One winter I led two bands, y'understand.

I love dancin', too. Calypsos, rhumbas, boleros, congas. I'm good at all. And jitterbug! Indeed, man! I am the best jitterbugger in Kansas City. When I played with the Monarchs and we was way ahead I would hit a double and jitterbug down to second. Good for the feet.

• • •

But the best leg exercise is playin' pool. I has walked thousands of miles 'round pool tables. Keeps my eyes sharp and keeps my pockets fulla change.

• • •

Huntin' helps the legs and I does lots of it. Quails,

jack rabbits and pheasants. I goes to Iowa and South Dakota for pheasants. The limit is three and I don't take no more 'cause that would be stealin'.

I collects shootin' guns and got one of the greatest collections in the world. Bought one on the road but Larry Doby, my Indians' roommate, made me sell it. "Big Leaguers don't carry guns," he told me.

• • •

I did some big game huntin' in the Blue Ridge Mountains.

Ain't going back there, though. Couple times some other hunters thought I was the game. I ain't hankerin' to be mounted on no mantel.

• • •

Like to fish, too. Catfish. Ain't nothin' better in the world than baked catfish. I got a secret recipe which I ain't lettin' out.

I always been special keen on automobiles. Most I ever had at one time was three cars, two trucks and two trailers. That was last year. I sold the car. Now all I got is a black Lincoln Continental and a blue Cadillac, a Chevrolet truck, a jeep and the two trailers. The truck's an army truck, with seats built in. I take the boys huntin' in it.

Stories has been written 'bout a shiny red Cadillac I has. I hasn't. Never did. Red's too bright. Had a maroon Cadillac, though. Bright maroon.

The first car I ever owned was a model T Ford. I drove it three miles backwards before it went ahead. Nobody told me 'bout the other pedal.

• • •

I ain't braggin' but it's true I got speedin' tickets in most every city in the U.S. Got twelve in Los Angeles in one month. Paid them all, too. The tickets are due to my clock trouble. I always realize I gotta be somewhere after I ain't.

• • •

That scar on my face I got in Birmingham. I was ridin' 'round the curve in a Chrysler Imperial I had. So was a truck. The other way, y'understand. My face needed eight stitches.

I'm also a photo fiend. Got four cameras and I took some shots of things other folks ain't never seen. I can get closer to different kindsa animals than most folks. Wish I'd taken a picture of that bowlegged jackass.

All the above is sidelines. My main hobby is antiques. The owner of the Monarchs, Mr. Wilkinson, his wife is in the business. She was tellin' me about a Chippendale once, and I asked, "What's his battin' average?"

Now I know 'cause I got a room filled with 18th century Chippendale furniture.

My main antique is a teakwood dinin' room set, complete, includin' six chairs. It showed at the Century of Progress. Cost me $3,000 and it's worth at least $5,000 now. I got the set in one room and it's restin' on a special $1,100 rug. Got two more $1,100 rugs.

• • •

I got lotsa antique chinaware, a $300 Meisin drinking stein, two English tankards, that's mugs, y'understand, and some other stuff I don't want to name 'cause you'd think I'm tryin' to show off.

• • •

I hadda buy a big house to keep my hobby. Got one with fourteen rooms in Kansas City at 220 E. 12th St., high on a terrace. Three friends stay there and take care of it for me. Got 65 chickens and a dozen dogs. Used to have 20. When I was with the Monarchs the boys used to board there free. Long as they didn't throw my antiques.

I got all kindsa tools—weldin' tools, pipe cutters, drills and all. Buy them all over the country. I am 'bout the best carpenter in the world. Also the best

electrician. Also the best plumber. You can call me a
"Botcher." I just go botchin' 'round. Last year I
changed all the pipes in the house. Just for practice,
y'understand.

I got a closet fulla shoes. Shoes I ain't never seen. I
got a closet fulla hats. Wear 'em once and drop 'em.
There is four closets fulla suits. Just ordered seven
suits from Ben the Tailor in Philadelphia. Nothin' less
than $75. Most near $150. The house is crawlin' with
neckties. Sure I is a Dude. Keeps me young.

• • •

**But the main thing is diet. Used to have a strict
one. Nothin' but fried food. Now I dassn't touch
fried. The doctors in Mayo Clinic heard my stomach
rumblin' and told me to eat only broiled and greens.**

• • •

I don't drink whisky, coffee or tea. Never did.
Nothin' but goat's milk, when I can get it. Some towns
has it. Some restaurants has it. But most hasn't. When
I can't get it I drink nothin' but hot water. Straight—
with sugar added.

I smoke cigarets and chew gum but no tobacco.
Once I took a chew in a game. I was reelin' drunk in
the second innin' and staggered to the clubhouse. I
quit right there.

Where I ruined my stomach was in Caracas, Venezuela in '37. At that time nobody there could say
"Bread," and I didn't know no Spanish words. I asked
for bread in a restaurant. All I got was a smile. The
man next to me said to the waiter. "Higado." They
brought him a plate of liver.

• • •

I said, "Higado." I got liver.
**I said "Higado" for two whole months. Breakfast,
dinner and supper. Nothin' but liver. My stomach**

started heavin' gas. Has been soundin' like "Old Fateful" ever since.

• • •

Now I can speak Spanish good. How I learned it was I met a girl in Caracas I kinda liked. Couldn't talk to her except if an interpreter was along.

Got rid of him in two weeks.

21
Still Learnin'

Since I joined the majors it's been one big thrill after another. The record-breakin' crowds makes me feel real good. My biggest thrill, though, was the first time I went nine innin's in the majors. That was in Chicago against the White Sox. [See Appendix C for box scores.] I blanked 'em 5–0. So many people come in to see the game they broke down two gates.

What I was most tickled 'bout was that folks hadda believe me at last. I always said it ain't no trick to go nine innin's. Not after a day or so of rest. Ain't nothin' to it.

Y'understand, I ain't never had rest before. 'Til I joined the Indians I was pitchin' every day. 'Course it was only three or five innin's 'cause I hadda travel from town to town with the Kansas City Monarchs and show in the lineup.

• • •

But three innin's is just like an appetizer. I pitched two innin's against the St. Louis Browns two nights before I went an easy nine against the White Sox.

• • •

To prove my pitchin' a full game was no fluke look what I did the next week. I beat the same White Sox [see Appendix C] again, this time, 1–0. They got only three hits and a record crowd was in the stands in Cleveland.

And I wasn't tired at all. I coulda gone another fifteen or twenty innin's either night and next day my arm was special fresh.

Y'understand when I go nine or more innin's I don't try to strike out nobody. Just give 'em all a piece of the ball so they pop up on the first or second pitch. No walks. No use wastin' time. But when I go in for relief, that's different. Then I go in for strikeouts.

'Till I came into the majors my most biggest recent thrill was when I went barnstormin' against Bob Rapid Feller's All-Star team the Fall of '47 on the coast. His team was made up of hand-picked American and National Leaguers.

Folks was sayin' then—like they said up 'till I beat the White Sox—I was only a three-innin' pitcher. Remarks like that always has been as irritatin' to me as havin' a nail in your shoe.

So I said to Bob Rapid, "You advertise a nine-innin' pitchin' duel between me an' you." He did and we played it in Wrigley Field, Los Angeles, November 3, 1947. My team win, 8–0. I breezed 15 of Bob Rapid's boys and give them but three hits.

It was great thrill to me 'cause they was All-Star major leaguers and I proved I could still pitch the distance.

• • •

Myself, I never thought I'd make the majors. I dreamed about it, of course, but I didn't figure it to happen.

• • •

Even when the Brooklyn Dodgers took Jackie Robinson from our Kansas City team three years ago and put him on their Montreal farm, I didn't think they was goin' to move him into the big leagues. Not 'til I saw his name in the lineup did I believe it.

When that happened I said to myself, "Satchel, don't you go lookin' at the big leagues. They ain't for you. They ain't goin' to meet your price and you ain't goin' to sign for no $5,000 like Jackie did."

I knew I wasn't, but I was tempted. 'Course I would

have been willin' to take a small cut. Real small. But nobody asked me.

When Mr. Bill Veeck signed Larry Doby in 1947 I figured maybe Mr. Veeck would look my way. I wrote him and he wrote back sayin' he didn't want to sign me 'cause folks might think it was a publicity stunt to attract customers.

This year when he didn't need the customers he called me—and I didn't get no salary cut.

I heard a lot about the majors all the years I was barnstormin'. It was nothin' like I heard. I heard there was goin' to be discrimination on the ball field. There ain't.

Everybody plays like brothers. I been treated like I been on the Indians for 20 years. I'm just one of the boys.

• • •

But the competition is somethin' like I ain't never 'sperienced in all the years I been 'round. The opposin' coaches try to rattle me, but they're just wastin' their time. Only man I listen to is Mr. Boudreau.

• • •

Now there is a great one, Mr. Boudreau. He is always thinkin', and thinkin' way ahead of the team we're playin'.

And Mr. Muddy Ruel and Mr. Bill McKechnie and Mr. Mel Harder—the coaches—have been great to work with. Always willin' to help. Maybe I been playin' longer than them, they still can teach me plenty. They have different kinds of signals up here— more complicated.

They been teachin' me a lot about the batters, too. Some I knew from barnstormin', but not the new ones. Wait 'till I study ALL the batters. Then if they hit me they got somethin' to talk about.

And remember I wasn't in tip top shape when I

joined the Indians. A pitcher ain't in shape 'till his legs are in shape. With the Monarchs I didn't need to be in shape. So I wasn't. Now it's different. I been workin' on my legs regular. When Mr. Veeck brought me to Cleveland for a demonstration before he signed me, I ran 'round the Stadium twice to loosen up and I shook my legs a special way. Then I was ready.

I been becoming readier ever since. Had a charley horse but I worked it out.

• • •

I ain't worryin' about my arm. It's always ready. just two hot baths a day and rub it with olive oil. My arm's goin' to last forever. It's my stomach that's wearin' out.

• • •

I figure my stomach will last another three to five years. Then it'll need upholsterin'. I figure I'll be pitchin' 'till that time.

When I retire from baseball, if ever, I'm goin' to buy a small chicken farm and spend my days.

After this season I'm goin' to do a little barnstormin' on the Coast. Then I'm returnin' to my home in Kansas City and do a little "botchin'." I'm goin' to build me one of the swellest rumpus rooms man ever created. All knotty pine.

But always my biggest thought will be to help the Indians win a pennant.

• • •

There is nothin' more I want than to win the pennant, and play in the World Series. I'd do anythin' to gain that.

Even tell my right age.

Appendix A

Unity Burial Association, Inc.
506 St. Michael Street, Mobile, Alabama

August 11, 1948

Mr. Hal Lebovitz
News Sportswriter
c/o Cleveland News
Cleveland, Ohio

Dear Mr. Lebovitz,

First I want to congratulate you on your articles concerning Satchel Paige . . . but may I make a correction which I believe will enlighten all the baseball fans throughout America concerning Mr. Paige's age. It is true beyond any contradiction that I gave Satchel his first chance to play professional baseball. I was the owner of the Chattanooga Black Lookouts of the Southern Association. It was in April 1926 that I carried him to Chattanooga for spring training. He was under age and I had to get permission from his mother to leave the city. Satchel was a great help the first year of professional baseball on our team. He enabled us to win the first half of the pennant. Then leaving our club in 1927 we sold him to Birmingham, of the Southern Association . . . He is somewhere (around the) age of 40, and what does age matter as long as you can produce the goods. Satchel Paige is a born pitcher and they don't make his kind every day. He will be a great help to the Indians. The Chattanooga Times may find in their files back in the year of 1926 some clippings of the home games we played there, for they would publish our league games with the full lineup of each game.

Mr. Stran Nicklin, who was president of the Chatanooga Lookout Club of the Southern League offered to give Paige $500 to pitch one Sunday game against the Atlanta Crackers of the Southern League, if he could get permission from the president of the league to pitch the game but because of his color he was rejected. I stated that year to let you see how good he was in the year of 1926.

May I tell you something of myself? I was a professional baseball player having an opportunity of playing with Gilkerson Union Giants of Spring Valley Illinois. I stayed in the big show five years from 1921 to 1925. Then I tried to be an owner in 1926 which I had a very successful year, then in 1927 I sold my interest out to a group of local men in Chattanooga, Tennessee. I went back to my club in 1927 through 1929.

After giving up baseball I went into the insurance business and am now the president and chairman of the board of directors of my company.

Hoping that this information that I have given you will clear the minds of all the doubting Thomases, and will start all to pulling for Cleveland to win the American pennant which would be a great honor to a great pitcher who was not given an opportunity to show how good he was in his hey day . . .

With best regards.

Sincerely yours,
(Signed) Alex L. Herman.

Appendix B

The following column appeared in the Cleveland News August 9, 1948. That night—after it appeared—Satchel Paige blanked the St. Louis Browns in a relief role for two innings. Two nights later he started against the Chicago White Sox and beat them 8–0. The writer Ed Bang, is the dean of midwest sport writers.

Between You and Me
By Ed Bang

I have known J. G. Taylor Spink since he was a mere youngster with no indication of hirsute adornment and unable to cast a vote. I knew his father before him. I have always had a great admiration for both father and son and to Taylor's credit it must be said he has made a wonderful publication out of *The Sporting News.*

However, I didn't subscribe to an editorial he wrote for his paper on July 14 and told him so. And now more than ever I insist Taylor went off the deep end to put into writing thoughts that came to him on the spur of the moment. It was the sort of editorial that could not possibly do him or his paper any good and that from a layman's standpoint was intended as a cruel thrust at a man of whom Cleveland and the entire United States—Bill Veeck—is justly proud.

I want to set forth a few excerpts from that editorial and then give some concrete information in rebuttal.

"Many well wishers of baseball emphatically fail to see eye to eye with the signing of Satchel Paige, super-annuated Negro pitcher, by Bill Veeck, publicity-minded head of the Cleveland Indians, to 'save the pennant for the Tribe.'"

"No man should set himself up against the achievement of another man's chances in life, be that man Negro or white, Chinese or Indian."

"Any criticism by this publication of the addition of Paige to the pennant-seeking forces of the Cleveland club obviously is not based on Paige's color."

"In criticizing the acquisittion of Satchel Paige by Cleveland, *The Sporting News* believes that Veeck has gone too far in his quest for publicity, and that he has done his league's position absolutely no good insofar as public reaction is concerned."

"Paige said he was 39 years of age. There are reports that he is somewhat in the neighborhood of 50."

"It would have done Cleveland and the American League no good in the court of public opinion if, at 50, Paige were as Caucasian as, let us say, Bob Feller."

"To bring in a pitching 'rookie' of Paige's age casts reflection on the entire scheme of operation in the major leagues."

"To sign a hurler at Paige's age is to demean the standards of baseball in the big circuits. Further complicating the situation is the suspicion that if Satchel were white, he would not have drawn a second thought from Veeck."

"William Harridge, president of the American League, would have been well within his rights if he had refused to approve the Paige contract."

First of all Taylor Spink should have had in mind exactly two things. He hires and pays salaries to men whom he thinks will be assets to his publication. Notwithstanding he is past 60 years of age he is still active in his line of duty and does a corking good job.

The same two things can be said of Veeck. He hires and pays big money in gambling on men who might become assets, and more money when they make the grade. Also he didn't give thought to Satchel Paige's age. It made no never mind to him whether Satch was

39, 44 or 47; whether he was Caucasian, Negro or Mongolian. He was honest in his conviction that Satchel would help the Indians and help them he did.

Let's review Paige's work for the benefit of my friend Taylor:

JULY 9—ST. LOUIS— FIFTH INNING—Stephens singled left. Priddy sacrificed, Berardino to Gordon. Platt fanned. Zarilla flied to Edwards. No runs, one hit. SIXTH INNING—Kokos singled center and took second on Judnich's fumble. Partee lined to Gordon who tossed to Boudreau for a double play. Pellagrini flied to Mitchell. No runs, one hit.

JULY 15—AT PHILA-DELPHIA—SIXTH INNING—Paige relieved Lemon, one run in and three on. Joost flied to Edwards. SEVENTH INNING—McCosky flied to Doby. R. Coleman fanned. Fain doubled right. Majeski hit home run on top of left field stand to tie score. Valo flied to Doby, Two runs, two hits. EIGHTH INNING— Franks fanned. Suder flied to Mitchell. Fowler flied to Doby. No runs, no hits. NINTH INNING—Joost flied to Mitchell. McCosky popped to Boudreau. R. Coleman singled left. Fain flied to Doby. No runs, one hit.

JULY 18—AT WASHINGTON—SIXTH INNING—Vernon flied to Clark, Kozar fanned. Evans walked. Haefner fanned. No runs, no hits.

JULY 19—AT WASHINGTON—EIGHTH INNING—Stewart singled right. Christman sacrificed. Paige to Gordon. Vernon was purposely passed. Kozar popped to GORDON. Stewart advanced on a wild pitch. Evans flied to Judnich. No runs, one hit. NINTH INNING—Wynn batted for Welteroth and fanned. Yost singled left. Coan rolled to Robinson. Gillenwater lined to Mitchell. No runs, one hit. TENTH INNING—Stewart doubled to short left. Christman was purposely passed. Zoldak relieved Paige.

JULY 21—AT NEW YORK—SIXTH INNING —Henrich fanned. Paige tossed out Berra. DiMaggio flied to Doby.

JULY 22—AT NEW YORK—SIXTH INNING —Byrne singled to left. Stirnweiss popped to Keltner. Henrich flied to Edwards. Keller forced Byrne, Gordon to Boudreau. No runs, one hit, SEVENTH INNING—DiMaggio fanned but reached first on Hegan's error. Niarhos sacrificed. Hegan to Gordon. Johnson fanned. McQuinn flied to Mitchell. No runs, no hits.

JULY 25—AT BOSTON —SEVENTH INNING— Dobson flied to Mitchell. DiMaggio hit a home run over left field wall. Pesky fouled to Hegan. Williams walked. Stephens flied to Doby. EIGHTH INNING—Doerr flied to Doby. So did Spence. Goodman walked. Tebbetts flied to Doby. No runs, no hits.

JULY 26—BOSTON— FOURTH INNING—Two runs in and Williams on first with one out. Stephens out, Boudreau to Robinson. Doerr fanned. No runs, no hits. FIFTH INNING— Mele grounded to Boudreau. Goodman and Tebbetts flied to Mitchell. No runs, no hits. SIXTH INNING—Galehouse out Robinson to Paige. DiMaggio doubled to right and took third on Clark's wild throw. Pesky flied to Clark, DiMaggio scoring, Williams bounced to Robinson. One run, one hit. SEVENTH

INNING—Stephens singled left. Doerr singled past Keltner. Spence popped to Keltner. Goodman singled left scoring Stephens. Tebbetts hit into double play, Gordon Boudreau to Robinson. One run, three hits. EIGHTH INNING— Boudreau threw out Galehouse. DiMaggio walked. Pesky flied to Mitchell.

AUGUST 3—WASHINGTON — FIRST INNING—Yost flied to Mitchell. Kozar walked. Coan also walked. Stewart tripled to left center scoring both runners. Vernon popped to Gordon. McBride popped to Boudreau. Two runs, one hit. SECOND INNING— Christman walked but was out stealing. Hegan to Boudreau. Earl and Wynn fanned. No runs, no hits. THIRD INNING—Yost struck out. Kozar singled center. Coan flied to Mitchell. Stewart beat out hit to Gordon. Vernon fanned. No runs, two hits. FOURTH INNING—Paige tossed out McBride. Christman fanned. Early flied to Clark. No runs, no hits. FIFTH INNING—Wynn doubled right Paige threw out Yost. Wynn holding second, Kozar beat out hit to Gordon. Coan flied to Mitchell. Wynn scoring. Stewart flied to Clark. One run, two hits. SIXTH IN-NING—Vernon beat bunt to Keltner. McBride flied to Doby. Kozar singled left. Early flied to Clark, Vernon going to third. Christman broke for second as Paige stepped on rubber but was out. Paige to Boudreau. No runs, two hits. SEVENTH INNING—Robertson flied to Kennedy in right. Yost fanned. Kozar walked. Coan popped to Keltner. No runs, no hits.

AUGUST 8—NEW YORK—EIGHTH INNING —McQuinn batted for Souchock and flied to Kennedy. Berra batted for Niarhos and flied to Kennedy. Rizzuto pop-singled center but was out stretching it, Doby to Berardino. No runs, one hit. NINTH INNING—Brown batted for Page and fouled to Hegan. Stirnweiss bunted safely. Paige balked. Henrich fouled to Robinson. Keller batted for Lindell and grounded to Gordon. No runs, one hit.

That adds up exactly to 10 games in which Paige has worked, Mr. Spink, a total of 26⅔ innings. He has allowed 23 hits, struck out 16, walked 10 and allowed seven earned runs. His record to date is THREE victories and ONE defeat. All this came to pass in one month.

Don't you think that calls for a broadminded editorial, Friend Taylor, explaining to all and sundry you were entirely mistaken about Bill Veeck signing Satchel Paige for publicity purposes and also admitting Paige still has enough in his pitching vocabulary to help any major league club? Also, Taylor, when it comes to publicity, let me ask you do you know many shrinking violets who steer clear of keeping in the limelight, not excluding yourself? Veeck may be a super de luxe individual when it comes to getting publicity but the guy knows his baseball as is well evidenced in the Satchel Paige, case, eh, what!

Appendix C

First Complete Game Friday, Aug. 13, 1948 at Comiskey Park

CLEVE.	A	H	O	A	Chicago	A	H	O	A
Mitchell,lf	4	1	5	0	Kol'way,2b	3	0	1	7
Peck,rf	4	1	2	0	Lupier,1b	4	0	11	0
Boudreau,ss	4	2	4	2	Appling,3b	4	2	1	1
E.Ro'son,1b	4	1	8	0	Seerey,lf	4	1	2	0
Gordon,2b	4	1	2	0	A.Rob'son,c	4	0	2	0
Doby,cf	4	2	3	0	Hodgin,rf	4	0	2	1
Keltner,3b	4	1	1	1	Philley,cf	3	1	6	0
Hegan,c	2	0	2	0	Michaels,ss	3	0	2	1
Paige,p	4	0	2	2	Gumpert,p	2	1	0	1
					*Wright	1	0	0	0
Totals	34	9	27	5	Moulder,p	0	0	0	1
					Totals	32	5	27	12

*Grounded out for Gumpert in eighth.

```
CLEVELAND ...  0 0 0 0 1 0 0 1 3—5
Chicago  ........ 0 0 0 0 0 0 0 0 0—0
```

Runs—Boudreau, E. Robinson, Doby 2, Keltner. Errors — Gordon, Kolloway, A. Robinson, Michaels.

Runs batted in—Hegan, Mitchell, Gordon, Doby. Three-base hit—Doby. Stolen bases—Doby 2, Hegan. Sacrifices—Kolloway, Hegan. Double play—Michaels, Kolloway and Lupien. Left on bases—Cleveland 4, Chicago 6. Bases on balls—Moulder 1. Struck out—Page 1, Gumpert 2. Hits—Gumpert, 7 in 8; Moulder, 2 in 1. Loser—Gumpert. Umpires — Passarella, Stevens and Rommel. Time—1:54. Attendance—51,013.

Second Complete Game Friday, Aug. 20, 1948 at
Cleveland Stadium

Chicago	A	H	O	A	CLEVE.	A	H	O	A
Hodgin,rf	4	0	3	0	Mitchell,lf	4	2	4	0
Lupien,1b	3	1	10	0	Clark,rf	3	1	0	0
Appling,3b	4	1	0	0	Kennedy,rf	0	0	0	0
Seerey,lf	3	1	1	0	Boudreau,ss	4	2	1	1
A. R'b'son,c	3	0	4	0	E. R'son,1b	4	0	8	0
Philley,cf	3	0	2	0	Keltner,3b	4	2	3	0
Kol'way,2b	3	0	4	4	Doby,cf	4	1	4	1
Michaels,ss	3	0	0	6	Ber'dino,2b	3	0	2	4
Wight,p	3	0	0	0	Hegan,c	3	0	5	0
					Paige,p	3	0	0	2
Totals	29	3	24	10	Totals	32	8	27	8

```
CLEVELAND ...  0 0 0 1 0 0 0 0 *—1
Chicago   .........  0 0 0 0 0 0 0 0 0—0
```

Run—Boudreau.
Run batted in—Doby. Two-base hit—Lupien. Left on bases—Chicago 3. Cleveland 8. Bases on balls—Wight 1. Paige 1. Struck out—Wight 4. Paige 5. Umpires—McKinley, McGowan and Boyer. Time—1:50. Attendance—78,382.

Index